Why Do You
Look at Me and
See a Girl?

GUERNICA WORLD EDITIONS 35

WHY DO YOU LOOK AT ME AND SEE A GIRL?

ANVI HOÀNG

GUERNICA
World
EDITIONS

TORONTO—CHICAGO—BUFFALO—LANCASTER (U.K.)
2021

Michael Mirolla, editor
Cover design: Rafael Chimicatti
Interior layout: Jill Ronsley, suneditwrite.com
Cover image by Trinh Mai: *Sữa Xưa* (Milk of Old), 2012 –
Acrylic, joss paper and hand stitching on canvas
Guernica Editions Inc.
287 Templemead Drive, Hamilton (ON), Canada L8W 2W4
2250 Military Road, Tonawanda, N.Y. 14150-6000 U.S.A.
www.guernicaeditions.com

Distributors:
Independent Publishers Group (IPG)
600 North Pulaski Road, Chicago IL 60624
University of Toronto Press Distribution,
5201 Dufferin Street, Toronto (ON), Canada M3H 5T8
Gazelle Book Services, White Cross Mills
High Town, Lancaster LA1 4XS U.K.

First edition.
Printed in Canada.

Legal Deposit—First Quarter
Library of Congress Catalog Card Number: 2020944503
Library and Archives Canada Cataloguing in Publication
Title: Why do you look at me and see a girl? / Anvi Hoàng.
Names: Hoàng, Anvi, author.
Series: Guernica world editions ; 35.
Description: Series statement: Guernica world editions ; 35
Identifiers: Canadiana (print) 20200324756 | Canadiana (ebook)
20200324764 | ISBN 9781771834452
(softcover) | ISBN 9781771834469 (EPUB) | ISBN 9781771834476
(Kindle)
Subjects: LCSH: Hoàng, Anvi. | LCSH: Vietnamese Americans—Biography.
| LCSH: Vietnamese American women—Biography. | LCSH: Vietnamese
American women—Social conditions.
Classification: LCC E184.V53 H63 2021 | DDC 973./00495922092—dc23

For Phan and Kat

CONTENTS

1. BEYOND

THE ROOM BECAME SMALLER WHEN the two women entered, a young lady and her mother. At forty-nine the latter already carried on her face all the stories life had to offer, a maelstrom of emotions. Her eyes sparkled light as much as they betrayed weariness. There was a certain calmness in the way she pressed her lips creating something like a smile. Once in the room, a musty smell penetrated her nose. A mixture of sweat, dust, and humidity in a space where the air stood still. It reminded her of the hustle-bustle and the stagnant air of a crowded city she had striven to stay away from. *Oh well, who would expect anything from this place*, she thought.

Some light came through a tiny window above her head. The fluorescent tube on the ceiling was on, but not bright enough to light up the place. As soon as the guard closed the door behind them, darkness flooded the room. Mother and daughter sat down on a bench underneath the window, keeping quiet. It was not exactly a place where people felt compelled to talk.

Very soon after that, a nun came into the room. The daughter greeted her with a slight smile, then turned to her mother and said: "Mom, here is the nun I talked to you about." The mother and the nun exchanged greetings. Their talking sliced open the stale air. Some normalcy was restored.

Not totally unexpected but a little abrupt from the casual conversation they had, the nun asked: "What is your name?" Something in the look of the mother prompted her to do so.

"Nguyễn Thị Cam," the mother replied.

* * *

Cam, in Vietnamese, means "orange" or "the color orange." Cam also is short for *cam chịu*, a concept that sometimes means "submission," other times "resigned to fate," and still others "endurance." Most of the time, its meaning derives from the combination of all three. It has a negative connotation and is often used to refer to people who are weak-minded. I find no English equivalent for it. But more importantly, Cam is my grandmother's name. She is my mom's mother.

The young lady is my aunt Hương, my mom's older sister. One summer afternoon in the cozy dining-room in her home in Đà Lạt, aunt Hương talked to me about this encounter between the nun and my grandma. There was something so provocative and upsetting about this story when the nun asked for my grandma's name that it became unforgettable to me. Going through black-and-white family pictures of the time, I could not help visualizing what the scene was like decades back.

My grandma Cam lived in Đà Lạt, an idyllic city in the mountains of the central highlands of Vietnam 186 miles north of Sài Gòn.

"One time, during the war, she came to Sài Gòn in one of her regular trips to visit her imprisoned children," aunt Hương recalled. When she showed up at the infamous Chí Hòa prison to see her son-in-law, aunt Hương's husband Phương, a Buddhist nun named H. Liên happened to be there for a similar reason. While waiting to see Phương, they talked.

"Something in the look of your grandma prompted the nun to ask for her name," aunt Hương's voice flickered. She did not want to show the emotion that flooded back as she revisited a tumultuous time in both her life and her mother's. "'Nguyễn Thị Cam,' your grandmother told her. At the end of the conversation, the nun gave your grandma the Buddhist name Ngọc Cam, and added: 'Cam here does not mean orange. It is short for submission.'"

I was shocked to hear the last sentence which I considered an insult. It was 1970. My grandma had been through French colonialism, the Japanese occupation during World War Two, and the upheavals of 1954 before the U.S.-backed Ngô Đình Diệm came to power. The country was divided into North Vietnam and South Vietnam. Grandma was immigrating from one city to another trying to settle her family down. She survived the bloodshed of the '68 Tết Offensive. More than ten years grappling with the American occupation in her own country, she survived in good spirit, doing her best to raise her family.

What on earth did the nun think she was doing, labeling my grandma 'submission'? I don't care if my grandma looked tired and beaten down. Hell, it was the sixties! Halfway around the globe, America was reeling from the war in Vietnam. Civil rights and anti-war protests were chipping the souls of American people. Right here in Vietnam, the drawn-out war seemed to have no end in sight. No Vietnamese soul was left untouched, young or old. I was furious to hear that the nun called my grandma submissive.

My grandmother had five children, two girls and three boys. Her oldest daughter, my aunt Hương, had spent months in a prison in Sài Gòn being interrogated and tortured for participating in anti-American, e.g. anti-government, protests. She was a Philosophy major and was working as a teacher at the time of her arrest. Aunt Hương has a deceptively demure appearance. Her porcelain skin is so smooth and her stare so gentle. Yet, she is not at all a mildly spoken person easily intimidated by anything or anyone. Her voice carried the clarity and determination unmatched and not-to-be-missed in its high registration. "Did you wash your hands before the meal?" she would often ask as we kids began to sit down around the dining table. Or "Don't put your feet on the table like that," she said casually as she passed through the living room where we were hanging out. Not that she raised her voice or anything. Hers is natural and burrows like a temple gong, effortlessly, echoing through the air for an ear to anchor in.

3

On holidays, she received gifts of cookies and candies, note-books and pens, clothes and scarves. In her bag, I would often see a couple of wool cones and an unfinished sweater spilling over the opening. She would give her nieces and nephews all those things she had and made and keep for herself a life of minimum posses-sion. After the death of her husband, she devoted her life to the revolution, work, and her family. She stayed with my grandma, raised a niece, and remained single all her life, ignoring all the men who had approached her over the years.

Beauty and passion remain with her. She stands tall like a statue upholding her integrity and dignity. I remember her as utterly self-less. After all, she is an original socialist-communist, one of those who followed Hồ Chí Minh's call. Because of her, while I was grow-ing up in the socialist-then-communist Vietnam, I often saw light in that clean-efficient-honest image of the officials even when I be-lieved only grayness and darkness surrounded us all. As long as I could remember, aunt Hương is a strong-minded woman, which explained the passion and courage I admired in her as a leader in the student movements in Sài Gòn in the 60s and 70s.

During her time in Chí Hòa, student protests became the main menu in the everyday life of Sài Gòn. The government could not ignore the demands to release the students' imprisoned colleagues. Facing increasing pressure, the South Vietnamese police eventually released aunt Hương because they did not have enough evidence to convict her. Aunt Hương's husband, Phương, who was also her comrade and supervisor, could not expect the same fate. Arrested at the same time with her, he was charged with possessing anti-government documentations and conducting anti-government activities. He was kept in Chí Hòa prison for many years, tortured, and eventually died there during the war.

The year earlier, 1969, Cam's husband, my grandfather, who used to work for the Ngô Đình Diệm government in the fifties be-fore he retired, specifically told their first son, my uncle Tuấn, to stay away from any revolutionary activities and just focus on finishing his degree in engineering. Sometime after that, my grandparents received news of his imprisonment in Sài Gòn for the very thing grandfather warned him not to do. The day Cam's second daughter, my mom, got married in 1969 was also the day her first son Tuấn was sentenced to twenty years imprisonment and sent to Côn Đảo prison in Côn Sơn island in southern Vietnam.

Sometime after 1970, Cam's second son, my uncle Hùng, was drafted into the South Vietnamese Army but he didn't report. He was soon captured and served a prison term in Sài Gòn for several months. At the end of the prison term, he was sent to the frontline far away from Sài Gòn up near the border with North Vietnam in Quảng Trị province.

The few years at the end of the sixties and the early seventies were the most devastating in grandma Cam's life. Between her various visits to the prison in Sài Gòn to see her oldest daughter and son-in-law, a part of her was in Côn Đảo with the first son, another part in Quảng Trị with the second son, still another part in Đà Lạt with her newly married daughter and the youngest 12-year-old third son who luckily was too young to be in any kind of trouble to tug at her soul. It was no surprise that grandma looked fatigued. With all the struggles, Cam's body and soul must have been wrenched dry from the tension. Yet, she was calm.

"Cam here is short for submission." I cannot help but think how inappropriate it was for the nun to have given my grandmother such a name, Ngọc Cam, and to have conveyed such a demeaning thought to her. I could feel that grandma was upset, her blood boiling in a sealed steel container making her unable to explode as she wanted to. But she could not afford an explosion anyway. Already too torn apart over her children to respond to a near-condemning comment from the nun, grandma remained mute to the insult.

That is how I imagine grandma's reaction. And that is a slice in my maternal family's story, one that was pretty typical among Vietnamese families at the time. In each family, there were always some older people who were born during French colonialism and grew up speaking French; there were younger others who were anti-French and thus supported the Việt Minh; many others later were captivated by communism; and still others who took the South Vietnamese government's side embracing capitalism, working with and for the Americans.

I see the same division in my paternal family.

Growing up observing this thread of family stories I learn that the constant conflict of ideologies within a family is a normal thing. It is a Vietnamese way of brewing new values into their daily tea for survival purposes. Vietnamese history of the nineteenth and twentieth century is strewn with all the wars and conflicts that were imposed upon its people forcing them to fight for survival, except their voluntary involvement in Cambodia in 1977. In the twentieth century alone, in total wars and war-related causes took the lives of more than eight million Vietnamese.

Most recently was the border hassle with the Khmer Rouge and their Chinese supporters in 1977. Government statistics quote more than one hundred thousand deaths from the battles. To middle-aged veterans who witnessed their friends fall in fire fight after fire fight, it feels like a million. And they believed the latter number to be correct.

The Vietnam War, or the Anti-American War as it is known in Vietnam, that ended in 1975, and its aftermath claimed more than four million Vietnamese lives.

The number of deaths from French colonialism is difficult to determine because it is a long period of time starting in the mid nineteenth century. The Indochina War, so-called in France, or the Anti-France Resistance War, in Vietnam, between 1946 and 1954 alone easily sent one million Vietnamese souls to the other world. Counting from the beginning of the twentieth century until the end of the Điện Biên Phủ battle in 1954, two million deaths is a conservative number. That is fifteen percent of Vietnam's then population of less than twenty million.

The famine at the end of the Second World War between 1944 and 1945 when the country was under the Japanese occupation gave rise to more than two million Vietnamese starving ghosts.

Eight million is not an exaggeration.

This history of Vietnamese deaths could be one way to explain why my life in Vietnam was like an inactive volcano of perturbation covered with equanimity on top, waiting to erupt. Under the surface are untold sorrow, unfathomable loss, unfulfilled promises, shattered dreams, unfinished business, broken contracts and so on. Peace does not seem enough to patch over the cataclysms. Borne out of bloodshed and bombing, Vietnamese people are obsessed about life as much as death. Racing with time, they have to catch up with both worlds. Hurry they live. Death they embrace. I often felt as if it was an existence where life and death embraced in a psychic dance to mock the living.

Throughout history, the unrelenting pressure to survive and the numbing tension to recover from ruins took over Vietnamese bodies, minds and souls. People rarely talked about anything else but survival. Most of the time the world around me as a child appeared as a cartoon in which the characters were mere shadows moving with pulled strings. In one scene, anchoring themselves in a survival mode, they hurriedly accepted what came their way; in another, they were nervously on the defense waiting for things to happen; in still another, they absorbed without questioning merely scurrying to find time to digest. Having been shadows for such a very long time, hundreds of years at least, they became shadowy sponges. Non-resistant absorbing became a tradition and we, most Vietnamese, lost our critical thinking.

There is no reason for me to get upset at the nun for calling my grandma 'submissive,' for such a condemning remark is 'just fine' in our culture. Many among us seem to replenish ourselves in an addiction to unload our angst and abuses onto our own kind. The way a once abused person turns to become an abuser in a vicious circle of life. Like an animalistic instinct—the very variance of the survival instinct that turns us into victims and perpetrators of our own.

I cannot tell exactly when I developed the fighting urges in me. It all started when I could feel that my mother was not completely happy and the other women around me also unhappy. A little child can always feel the most delicate pulsations in the mother's heart without the need for vocal communication. I knew her hectic life around the four children like us was not cause for unhappiness.

Every day, in our small space in the house in Sài Gòn, the five of us would be on bed. We lay, we sat, we surrounded her. Picture books in hand. "Read *Beauty and the Beast* mom!" "No, let's read *Tin Tin*, mom!" "No, I prefer *The Steadfast Tin Soldier*!" We would scream. Those books are large in size, two times our head, in either English or French, the smooth colorful pictures in them dreamy. Mom would read all of them before we agreed to go to bed. Her enchanting voice kept the house safe and sound as we tumbled into our dreams.

"Do you know that your mom was the most beautiful girl in Đồng Khánh high school?" cousin-uncle Lễ's voice echoed. My mom's face shines brightly. She has light complexion. Unlike many of us, she has high-bridged nose she inherited from her father's side. "Every afternoon after school," he would continue, "a long line of boys would tail her from outside the school gate all the way to our home. Your uncle Thưởng and I had to be her bodyguards. Even to this day, her skin is as blush and smooth like nobody else." He ended his sentence with the sense of triumph of a big brother. That actually was not a dream. Cousin-uncles Lễ and Thưởng are four or five years older than my mom. They grew up together in Huế and have remained close over the years even with geographical distance between them, they living in Huế and my mom in Sài Gòn. Whenever uncle Lễ came to visit us he often talked about their childhood and never forgot to mention how beautiful my mom was and still is. He did not need to remind me of that. All my friends from elementary school to college, after meeting with my mom the first time would gasp with a big exclamation mark: "Your mom is so beautiful and kind!" Their eyes almost rolled up to touch their browses as they told me. And they told me so over the years.

I did not understand, as a child, how a woman so intelligent, pretty and regal and who always smelled fresh like the tropical rain as she did could not find happiness to her heart's desire. "Beautiful" and "kind" were always together in my friends' comments. I thought about the two words as curses on my mom, things that were reserved for outsiders to bestow; things that brought misery to my mom at home; as if because she was beautiful and kind, she possessed more talents than others to be condemned.

A typical house in Sài Gòn elongates both in height and length on a narrow piece of land thirteen feet wide. Ours is almost twenty feet. A fortune in others' eyes. Inside that multi-story house, my family lived with my father's father on the middle level (my paternal grandmother died when I was four). My aunt's family of eleven occupied the ground and top floors. Next door on the back was my other aunt's family of eleven. We literally shared the back wall through which we made a hole and put a door to it so we could go from my house to hers like one titanic mansion. Two minutes' walk away could be found my other aunt's family of six. There are six in our family plus my grandfather. Altogether, that was one gigantic family.

Sometimes after dinner, my mom, my sister, and I would sit around on the wooden floor, our hands pruny inside the wall of a big plastic basin full of beans totally submerged in water. They were white Hyacinth beans for *chè đậu ván*. It is a lot of work to prepare this dessert but always worth it—I don't know anyone who does not love it. Eyes on the beans, we moved our hands in and out of the water. The gently splashing sound as the back of our hands pressed down the surface to scoop the beans out was soothing. S-p-l-a-s-h, s-p-l-a-s-h, s-p-l-a-s-h. It made the talking up and down and around us fade. Some kid upstairs would drop something thudding on the wooden floor. Sometimes I even thought that is the sound of death, a very violent death. We were living in a house where the number of kids totaled a dozen plus, more than enough to form a soccer team. Breaking things and chasing and wrestling were part of the everyday energy of life. S-m-a-s-h! A glass shattered as it hit the tile floor downstairs. Another person must be leaving this world with a big bang. Life and death on different floors, under the same roof.

S-p-l-a-s-h. They became irrelevant noises of our life.

There were only three of us with a mountain of beans. After we pealed their skin, the clean beans reveal their true yellow color. Once cooked, the two halves of the bean split, most of them do. Later on, in the sweet thickened translucent base of tapioca flour mix topped with a spoon of coconut cream white as cotton flower, these floating beans the shape of rubber leaves melt like butter in the mouth. Right now, they gleamed in the two bowls on the sides of the basin. In the space in front of our feet, three piles of shell were rising.

"But why are there so many beans, mom?" I asked.

"Tomorrow is great great grandfather's death anniversary," she said. "The big family alone is over thirty people. Then we have tons of guests as well. That's a lot of people to cook for. We need a lot of *chè*."

My mom had a sweet voice. Like most Asians, it is on a high range of pitch. Even when she speaks softly, it is ringing warm like amber.

Two hours later, I looked and realized we went through only half of the bean mount. My sister and I were already tired.

"Go to bed," my mom told us. "I'll finish up."

The sweet experience working with mom began to burn up like raging fire in me. I knew it would take her many more hours to finish the beans. And *chè* was one of the dishes she had to cook. Tomorrow, she would have to get up very early to go grocery shopping for the event. The local market is three minutes away on foot. Sometimes my sister or I went along to help her carry things back home. Sometimes she took two or three trips back and forth to haul up all the merchandise. Then the whole day would be one exhausting string of activities hung around her neck. To survive and to belong, she wore it like a jewel. It left her struggling to catch a breath.

Since I could begin to think a little, I often resented the fact that as a beautiful and capable wife of the oldest son in the big family, my mom was obliged to work harder than others at death anniversary parties. Juggling her teaching job, taking care of the six of us plus my grandfather, living in an extended family, and fulfilling family anniversary obligations, she became skinny like a yellow thinking reed. Sometimes I saw her sit by the dining table and inhale deeply, her belly curving in and making such a big hollow I wanted to put my head there to fill up the emptiness. At those times, I could feel her gaze towards nothingness. It was heavy.

Since those early days, I could see how claustrophobic it was to be bound by traditions, and how far back we stayed where traditional thinking kept us. Traditions impeded any alternative vision I might have of the future. *There must be a different way to live.*

I did not see a bright future around, in the conversations between my newly wed cousins and the 'expert-married-women' in the big family. Every time they hung around, they gossiped about their husbands. "Men," the older ones philosophized, "are all the same. We cannot change them." Others would nod in agreement. They talked about how chauvinistic their husbands became, totally different from the gallant guy who courted them the earlier years. "Good luck asking him to help with any housework! Look at me as an example. It is faster for me to do it myself than to wait for him," the experienced ones would comment, breaking a perfunctory more than blessed smile. "Enjoy your honeymoon while it lasts," they concluded with a familiar statement. This is common advice given at some point by the older women as proof of their matrimonial experience and "wisdom" to the newlyweds. The sureness and righteousness in the way they expressed it made it sound as if the honeymoon was the only happy moment in one's marriage, and even though it was brief it was also the only path to some possible happiness in life.

Maybe marriage was that way for them. Maybe marriage was the only way for them to go through life.

What they could not hide from me was the disappointment and bitterness in their tone. It soaked like a sorrowful ferment in my stomach. I felt sorry for them, but was more confused by the acceptance in their attitude. "Why did they have to get married to be complaining later?" Unable to make sense of the adult world and not accepting the confusion in behaviors around me, the child in me started asking silent questions, naively. Together with accumulative ignorance about the complexity in human behavior and society and everything else that happened in the world outside Vietnam, I continued, as I grew older, to stick to my simple, obvious questions phrased in a way that I now know would bring me more enemies than friends: "We live in the twentieth century. Isn't living about making life better—as we move along—a goal for all human beings? Isn't each decision we make supposed to get us to a better state in life? Otherwise, why make the move at all?!" The militant tone is the legacy I picked up while cohabiting in a dysfunctional family with the five terminators: Confucianism, colonialism, imperialism, capitalism and communism.

During my life in Vietnam, I never stopped thinking about the solutions to the issues I raised for myself. Around me, in the name of survival and belonging, or to put it in a more 'appropriate' way, to maintain 'harmony,' the Vietnamese adults wore their disgruntle around their neck like jewelry. Their tales of harmony and survival are merely covers for blind acceptance and self-destruction. They tested my patience and pushed me to the edge of a rebellion against traditional thinking. Hanging there for a long time, I craved for new ways to look at life and to obtain more meaning from it.

I knew too well how tough life after the war was. But I also felt that, at least in peacetime, the situation was stable enough to push forward my belief that life should move beyond the basics of food and shelter. It should be about something bigger than oneself. (I was blindly idealistic, yes.) We did not exist in war literally, not in the sense of bombings falling and death all around us like a twentieth century apocalypse. But it was war nevertheless, war on mental and psychological levels. Humans need to face themselves and to battle the surrounding establishment. I knew early on that challenging dominant forces around me was the only way to free myself from the grip of traditions and thus find some measure of happiness.

The struggling and searching continued for many years. I carried them with me in my decade-plus years of life in the U.S. They dried out, they rehydrated, they withered, they plumped up. They recycled their life and transformed their energy. Until they blossomed into a determination. All the stories of struggles and survival of Vietnamese women I used to simply take all in, and sometimes be a part of—both as a victim, and a perpetrator by retelling them the expected way—are not enough anymore. Not because those stories are mono-dimensional but more because the storytellers could not grasp more than that. Or they did not want to read more from them. Or they did not have a chance to do differently. How abundant the narrators are—Vietnamese, Vietnamese descents, non-Vietnamese. Their portrayal of Vietnamese reality is infested with narratives of survival. It not so much reflects a grain of truth as it reveals thriving space for patronization and victimization, the very elements of fertile ground to nourish inequality and injustice.

If anything, their stories failed me. While there are various ways to tell stories, the only way that soothes my soul is for the author to cast out from the story an energy that creates life anew, not just to survive but to be visible and to rise.

If anything, the narrators forget that to stress survival is to forsake a crucial message the very survivors mean to send: excel. They made sacrifices so that their children and grandchildren and great-grandchildren could fly.

That is Inspiration, the only thing that could grow the seed of life in me. The passage of time only cements my belief that surviving was not inspirational enough anymore. For my own salvation, I have to debunk a very established tradition which many, starting with Vietnamese people, still hold tightly as they turn to judge women in my grandma's generation, and even my mother's: They consider women 'home-bound,' 'submissive' and 'resigned to fate.'

This viewpoint reflects a very outdated Confucian teaching that upholds a man's position and praises male scholars indiscriminatingly. In the old days, while it bestowed men with all privileges, it belittled Vietnamese women, stripping them of an education and human rights. Confucianism was useful two thousand years ago in times of chaos to establish order, to squash individualism-creativity-and-progress. It should not be used in a modern country like Vietnam in search of a way to revitalize and to move forward. The current Vietnamese belief in a hierarchical society that does not question authority nor old traditions and that respects seniority above anything else is choking any life left out of a country so old yet so young with unrelenting makeovers.

I now openly condemn that backward Confucius point of view. Not that Vietnamese people talk about it daily. Many of them may not be aware of what Confucianism is or that their behavior is undoubtedly following Confucius. It is already a part of their DNA. I want Vietnamese people to recognize this in order to get rid of it.

My re-interpretation of my grandma Cam getting agitated at the nun's comment is my own. Maybe my mom, aunt Hương, my uncles and many other relatives do not see grandma the same way I do. But I live in the twenty-first century and see the world differently. In my view, grandma Cam was among the most fascinating women I have known. All her life, she aimed for the best. With the flexing bow of decision in hand, she drew one arrow of survival. For the rest of the bundle, she shot out her envisioned dreams—the dreams that I share, along with millions of people on the planet, and strive to achieve.

"Grandma, why did you let my mom, uncle Tuấn and aunt Hương go far away for high school while local schools were just as adequate?" I asked. We were picking chayote in the garden. These thin-skinned beauties hanging above my head in the vines are as big as an adult's hand. They love the cool weather of Đà Lạt so much they grow almost like weeds there. Their light green flesh bulges up and shines through. Fresh chayote, sliced paper thin you can see through when held up against the sun, stir-fried with only garlic and fish sauce, is good enough to bring back all the sweetest memories. Chayote cubed and simmered in a broth of carrot and fatty pork shoulder wins over the

most difficult Vietnamese eaters. No Vietnamese I know can refuse this kind of slow-cooked soup. I folded my arm close to my side and began to stack the chayote lengthwise. The scent of freshness filled the air. Even the soil in grandma's garden smelled fresh. Mixing all that into my mom-and-aunt Hương-and-uncle Tuấn's-away-from-home high school journeys, I had an intoxicating cocktail.

"Don't you remember the saying?" Grandma's voice disrupted my daydreaming. "Travel broadens the mind. I also believe that one has a right to knowledge and a right to live their life as they wish. With knowledge and understanding people tend to be less mean and cruel. Life will be pleasant for us all."

"During the war when aunt Hương, uncles Tuấn and Hùng were in jail for their antiwar activities, how often were you allowed to visit them?" I asked, thinking about how distraught and miserable she was, and how she could easily have become in such a situation a whining, helpless, depressed and neglected wife and mother. Then the lone journeys she made on the road from the furthest southern corner of the land, Côn Đảo island, up to the northern edge of South Vietnam in Quảng Trị province, bringing love to the children of war.

"I was so worried then, my heart ached all the time," grandma said. "But to be their faithful supporter is the best I could do. They were adults, made their own decisions in life and had to follow them through. I believed that their strength, the same one they used to pursue their ideals and passions, would help them triumph over their own ordeals to reach the destination of their choice, whatever it was. Around once a month, I am allowed to see them. It took weeks to move from one place to another." Grandma's face lifted and her eyes aimed at the dangling chayote right above us. Grabbing a big one by the bottom, she twisted it around its stem. After three rounds the stem began to thread away and readied to sever from the vine. One last gentle twist and the lime green beauty nestled coolly in grandma's palm.

"And grandma, how come you never interfered in their love life? You never told them to date or not to date someone?" Grandma looked right into my eyes. Her lips slowly broke into a smile.

"Well, I believe in freedom in love. Don't you, con?"

Survival is doing the best expecting the worst.
Inspiration is aiming for the best.
And so the stories of my grandma unfold.

2. CAM

M Y GRANDMOTHER CAM WAS BORN in 1921 in the city of Huế. For close to a century and a half, under the Nguyễn dynasty (1802-1945), Huế was the imperial capital of Vietnam. The French occupied Vietnam in 1862 and divided the country into three parts: the protectorates of Tonkin and Annam in the north and center, respectively, and the colony of Cochinchina in the south. The court became a nominal force. The Emperor resided in Huế in the central part. The formal and feudal way of life continued to be the standard of living in Huế as it had been since the eighteenth century.

Huế is a small city with a huge reputation as the most beautiful and poetic in the land. Its residents are blessed with Sông Hương, Perfume River, running through the city as a pheromonal scarf ready for a whirlwind from the Ngự Bình mountain on the city's southeastern side blowing in to ribbon itself around one's neck. Everywhere around the city, the view of the river and the mountain could be obtained from high ground. They chase each other in a preamble to the courtship for the attention of every Huế resident.

Early mornings the fifteenth day of the month, the billowing fog rising from the river will roll into the descending mountain wind and melt into the vibrating thousand-year-old temple gongs edging forward toward the least celestial corner of their residents' human souls. Everyday contemplation in the presence of long ornately robed court mandarins, awakened by pagoda chanting and surrounded by the mystic secrets of their beloved river and mountain, Huế residents learn manners, a sense of culture and spirituality early on. The natural and humanistic endowments imbibed in them an iconographic memory and feeling of the place, one bonded to the city's ancient imperial history. They carry those with them everywhere they go. Vietnamese people elsewhere often think about those born and raised in Huế as more refined, for a good reason.

Yet, only Huế people can describe how the freezing damp air shakes hand with the heavy rainfall to pierce their bones during the winter months.

Huế is a land of imperial palaces and tombs, forlorn moss-embossed graveyards of eunuchs, and antique three-quartered houses. A walk around to the roomy back yard of these houses would land you into oblivion. The dirt path along the side of the house leads past a lotus pond, folds itself around a star-fruit tree before directing you to the furthest corner of the yard. You emerge in the quiet presence of a tomb, or two. The air is still, stirred only by the occasional cicada singing. These traditional houses were nothing but designated private settings where many generations share their spaces both in life and death.

In June and July, hot dry wind from Laos plunges through the mountain range, picks up its temper and dumps its broiling air onto Huế. This brazen heat skews ones along on a stick of human flesh marinated by a bizarre flavor of droughty elemental particles and a dash of the musty vestigial sense of death very distinctive of Huế. One could become sick from it, or pixilated by the position of time and space right where one is. The sensibility is especially real around the week of Lost Souls Ceremony. According to the lunar calendar, it is the twenty-third day of the fifth month of the year, which is the end of June or early July. In Western calendars, it marks the massacre that happened on July 5 of 1885. Thousands of Huế residents were killed on this day when French soldiers attacked the city. Their body counts laid the foundation for the French colonialism that was about to be complete. Bodies of mandarins, soldiers, or civilians young and old, whether hanging over a high wall, strewing the streets, or bloating in a pond, were buried together in mass graves. The government erected a shrine to commemorate the event and Huế people have been praying for those deaths ever since.

On the late afternoon of June as the heat subsides the incense arises. Make-shift outdoor altars are raised in front of every house. On the cloth-covered table lie in abundance food, fruits, and flowers. The sun goes down and light fades. Throughout the alleys and along the streets people begin to light up their bowl of incense sticks and burn paper offerings. Flickers of fire go off and soon fill up the darkness. It is unexpectedly quiet, and somber. Ashes from incense and burned paper fly about on the asphaltic surface diddling around your ankles everywhere you walk; ashes in the air scented of sorrow and silvered by the fading light like ghosts. It could be a shivering sensation.

This event is for Huế only, not to be confused with the Daoist Ghost Festival celebrated in Vietnam and other Asian countries on the fifteenth day of the seventh month each lunar year.

And it happened again during the Tết Offensive Massacre in 1968. Huế people saw some six thousand souls off joining the realm of the un-living right before their eyes, or around the corner. People were ordered to dig their own graves and climb into them. They were buried alive.

The dead and the living in Huế have shared a susceptibly porous presence for centuries. The sizzling summer temperature does more than sear the surface.

Local people often recount both the cold and the heat in Huế as nasty beyond description. They learn to survive and work hard to retain their foothold.

My grandma Cam was born and grew up in this city.

She was the first of ten siblings. When Cam was nineteen, her father said that he had found a husband for her, a well-educated and very kind man. In this predetermined way, Cam was handed a husband, my grandfather Tín, whom she married in 1940. The marriage was considered socially compatible and highly desirable as both families held the same social status.

Born into a progressive peasant family from Phú Long village, Bình Định province, in 1903, Tín was sent to school together with three of his brothers. Education was a long and strenuous journey at the time because the colonial French government specifically designed it that way to impede literacy and learning for the native population. In modern language, it is the K-13 French system. The brothers finished sixth grade and received a certificate, a Primaire as the locals referred to it. While two of them chose to become village teachers, Tín went on to a bigger city, Quy Nhơn, where high school education was available, to study more. He completed the tenth grade and got a Diplôme.

In the 1930s, it was extremely hard and very rare for people from provinces or villages to pursue education. This huge accomplishment, therefore, secured him a prestigious social status, and a great job, not to mention a grandiose welcome-home ceremony from his native town. "The day he came back," said aunt Hương, "the villagers carried him in a palanquin followed with a big crowd in a procession."

The image of a palanquin immediately transposed me. My mind began to wander towards the familiar scenes and details I have seen in Đông Hồ woodblock paintings and read from textbooks. A mandarin in embroidered silk garment sits comfortably in his chair. Around him, colorful village flags in various bright colors fly in the air. It's supposed to be hot all the time in Vietnam but in the prints and the books, the air seems to be so cool and nice. Heavy humidity also makes it rare for the flags to fly the way they do in print.

Everybody looks happy, even the carriers with the weight on their shoulders. Far away, there must be another crowd waiting to congratulate him at the village. Some are busy setting up tents. Others chasing the pigs and the chickens they are supposed to prepare for the grand meal. The children are right behind them, laughing at the chase. Somewhere in the kitchen, bundles of greens are washed. Pots of water boiled. And pans oiled. Already, the smell of food begins to attract people up and down the village, even the lazy ones who are taking their mid-day nap. Then the whole village partakes of a feast that lasts days.

How glamorous, I thought. Those things did happen to my grandfather, aunt Hương confirmed and brought me back to reality, just in time to deliver me into another dream. "To honor him," she continued, "they also presented him with a pair of wooden plaques." These were vertical so that the villagers could inscribe gold-plated words of congratulations. According to aunt Hương, "these plaques are still hanging on the wood pillars in the living room of the ancestral house in Phú Long, Bình Định."

With the degree, to make a living grandfather Tín chose to become a 'mandarin' of the French colonial government. In 1936 he started work as an administrative officer in the Protectorate of Annam located in Huế. People began to address him as Ông Phán, loosely translated as Mr. Diplôme, implying his Diplôme degree and his position in the French administration. This is who he was when he married grandma Cam. The Protectorate of Annam was the French administrative bureau with authority over and management of the whole central area of Vietnam including the court.

So he spoke French well. I could hear myself saying out loud excitedly as aunt Hương was telling me about grandfather and his job. This little detail about his involvement in the French bureau triggered a nostalgia in me about a past where a marriage between a 'French mandarin' and daughter of a court mandarin was great celebratory news. Wait. What did I just do? Or did I do it again? *It is irresistible to fantasize the past.* Growing up under communism, my familiar vocabularies were words such as workers, farmers, labor and victory, communist party, union and socialist, ration, co-operatives and youth union, etc. All around and ahead of me, the present and the future were misty at most (more about this later).

Having nothing to look forward to, the past became an alluring force. The kid in me have to admit that this little discovery about grandpa speaking French added spice to the whole story of grandma and grandpa that I could not resist envisioning. As I pondered grandma Cam's life up till her marriage, the practical and socialist parts in me yearned for what was missing in my colorless childhood. I felt smitten by the fairytale-like story of her marriage as all the details appeared so surreal. A simple word like 'mandarin' or 'Diplôme' could create the equivalent Disney effect of magic on me. As a grown person, I still find myself doing it even as I criticize the whole thing as feudalistic, colonialistic, or imperialistic, and deplorable.

The past is a trap most of the time. You will always leave out someone or something while being busy festooning your own. I realized there were no women in the picture of my grandfather in a palanquin. The truth is in feudal and colonial times most of them were not allowed to go to school; if any dared to write at all they were not published; they were tucked away in the kitchen corners. Just to mention a few oppressions.

And sometimes it is a sin.

I did not grow up speaking French. Nor was I face to face with a living French person growing up. We did not even learn French literature at school. Yet, somehow I absorbed enough French aura in the environment to feel nostalgic about the past French presence in Vietnam. The French soldiers and bureaucrats did not come to Vietnam on a humanitarian mission. Millions of Vietnamese died during French colonialism from starvation, torture, rape, slave labor in the rubber fields, in prisons, or on battlefields. And here I am fantasizing that past.

I know that is the mentality of an enslaved subject who resisted their master as vehemently as they aspired to the power he embodied. It's an ancestral sin transferred to me as a curse. Somewhere deep inside, I must reverberate to the French influence, whether I want it or not. I know some Vietnamese don't understand this, or refuse to. Many others do not believe nor accept it. Regardless of their reactions, the enslavement of its subjects by the French colonialists is a historical fact and the French allure in Vietnam is still so real.

What is also real is the fact that the curse passes from generation to generation. Just look at how Vietnamese people are especially hypnotized by French-ism—anything French is glittering in their eyes. They worship the culture and the cuisine, and they are help-lessly cultic about the literature. The sound of the French language does not fail to lull them into distant dreams. This mentality must be rooted in the paramount European culture mesmerization, like nothing else. Even when American culture is dominant in Vietnam nowadays, the French appeal still has its own way of cozying up with everyday life.

Getting out of big cities like Sài Gòn and Hà Nội, in whichever direction you choose, you will witness spectacles that are proof of this mostly deformed love affair between French and Vietnamese cultures. Small cities in the countryside are sites where conflicted memories manifest themselves in the most obnoxious ways, like a halfway house between heaven and hell. As a tentacle of globaliza-tion reaches these small cities, changes rush in. Business grows, or money—received from relatives in the U.S. hard-earned from their sweat and sent over out of love, guilt, or pride, as Hưng Cẩm Thái discussed in his book *For Better or Worse*—becomes abundant. People begin to plan for a life of pleasure and romance. Lo and be-hold, nothing is better to meet their desire for something glorious and poetic (the Vietnamese love poetry) than a French villa. In the middle of nowhere, rising up from the rice fields, a mansion with columns and front balconies in elaborate decoration. I could see their curves half a mile away. All the mansions are in bright colors of green, blue, orange or yellow. That is the local interpretation of French architecture.

The French allure manifests in small-scale and edible objects as well where there are more flabbergasted notes than one can sing. A sliding door is luxurious and modern, but a French door is classic and elegant. Ham is trendy, but *jambon* is gourmet and classy. *Iron Chef* is so cool, but a *sous-chef* is irresistible. Life sucks, but *c'est la vie* is philosophical. The French appeal is real. So much so that many educated Vietnamese even think that French colonialism did good for the Vietnamese and it should have stayed put for another hundred years. I would not go that far. Enough is enough. I was surprised nonetheless to observe the French appeal working in me. And I am on guard constantly. If a public confession would do the trick, I hope it rids me of it.

That aside, I could not change the fact that, back then, the marriage between grandpa Tín, a 'French mandarin,' and grandma Cam, daughter of a court mandarin, was great celebratory news.

My great-grandfather, grandma Cam's father, was himself a well-educated man and a court mandarin. He started working for the court in Huế at the beginning of the twentieth century, in 1910, during the Nguyễn Dynasty under Emperor Khải Định. After Khải Định died, he continued to work for Emperor Bảo Đại until the last day of this last emperor of Vietnam. His main concern in life as an elder son was to support his big family including his mother and his siblings.

Great-grandfather was well-known and much respected in Huế, not only because of his court position but also his major hobby. With advanced knowledge and skill in herbal medicine, great-grandfather spent a lot of time outside the court helping to cure illnesses for everybody around him. When his first wife died after giving birth to two children, he remarried. My grandma Cam was the first child of the second wife.

As daughter of a mandarin, everything in grandma Cam's life sounded like a dream. And maybe to outsiders looking in, happiness and prosperity seemed to encircle her like a wreath.

Except that Vietnam was under French domination then. Since 1884, the colonialists maintained a dual system of French and Vietnamese administration in the North and Central parts of the land with a nominal Emperor residing in Huế. Growing up in this imperial city, Cam never liked the feudalistic thick air of rules and traditions that seemed to compress its dwellers into mementos or miniatures in a museum model. She often described it as stagnant to aunt Hương.

Together with several other siblings in the family, Cam embraced the new ideas. They loved novels and stories by modern writers and novelists of the early twentieth century such as Nhất

Linh and Khái Hưng who founded, in 1932, a group called "Self-Strengthening Literary Group." This group took the country by storm with their criticism of the outdated feudalistic values. In their stories, they portrayed mothers-in-law as near monsters who came between the son and his wife. Young husbands who lived under the mothers' spell and took their side against their own wives were nothing more than weaklings. Nhất Linh and Khái Hưng also condemned the traditional obligations that bound the women to the men and their families. They professed and promoted freedom in love, equality, as well as liberty, in ways nobody had ever seen before, using modern Vietnamese language. Cam loved this kind of literature.

Anti-French movement never ceased to exist in the country. In the 1940s it was strongly revived with widespread and grassroot organization of the Việt Minh. At this same time, the Second World War was going on and the political situation in Vietnam was very unstable with the Japanese occupation.

During the Second World War, Japan emerged in the global scene with its pan-Asian coalition. Tokyo looked to Vietnam as a vassal state providing cheap land, labor and resources and began to pressure the Indochinese administrators. In June 1940 the French government's surrender at home to Berlin naturally weakened the position of the colonial government in Vietnam. The colonialists had to concede to the Japanese demands of rights and interests in South-East Asia and allowed Japanese troops total access to Vietnam. The new rulers removed the French from real power and made them work for the new force. On the streets of Huế, it was now Japanese soldiers that terrorized the Vietnamese. From fighting against the French, the Việt Minh coalition turned to oppose Japan. Their goal remained to gain freedom for the country from whichever enemy it faced.

All these ideas and movements greatly affected Cam. They instilled in her hope of independence and equality, issues that she and her brothers talked about all the time. Other than that, happiness was an illusion to Cam. She said to her father that she did not want to get married. Deep down, she believed in love, and a pre-arranged marriage is nothing of the sort. I don't think grandma told my great-grandfather in so many words her thoughts on the issue, but she did tell him she didn't want to be married off. To which he responded: "I'm sick and cannot take care of you all. To have you married off is having some responsibility taken off my shoulders. Please accept the proposal."

Even some daughters in the twenty-first century would find it difficult to say "No" to such a request from a father. I understand why grandma Cam agreed to the arranged marriage.

* * *

Between 1941-1945 the Japanese occupation force used the French administration to run the country so they could save some of their own resources and soldiers. Then, in March of 1945, on the verge of losing the Second World War, the Japanese officers in Vietnam decided to carry out a coup d'état against the French and took total control of the country, because Tokyo envisioned Vietnam to be a fallback location for retreating Japanese troops. The Second World War was drawing to an end and Japan, shocked and attacked on all fronts including the bombing of Hiroshima and Nagasaki, was on the hot seat. When the Japanese surrendered to the Allies in early August, the Việt Minh seized the opportunity of disarmed French troops and a weak occupation force to topple the Japanese and take over.

In Huế, Grandma Cam embraced the swift victory of the Việt Minh as she would a light Spring breeze that swept away the hot summer wave. She enjoyed the country's freedom and independence. But it was only temporary. No long after, with assistance from the United States, the French restored their rule in Indochina, included the central and southern parts of Vietnam, yielding the North to the Việt Minh.

In 1946, without enough manpower to hold on to Huế in the central region, the Việt Minh force had to withdraw to the free zones, paving the way for the return of French control in Huế for another eight years. Before leaving, the Việt Minh had had enough time to reassign my grandfather and many others in the Protectorate of Annam administration to work for them in the Committee of Resistance and Administration of South Centre in the liberated zone of Bồng Sơn in Bình Định province further south of Huế.

The conflicts made traveling from place to place almost impossible, especially between a French-controlled area and a Việt Minh zone. Grandma's enthusiasm was cut short when the French restored their rule in Huế and grandfather was stuck in liberated Bồng Sơn with the Việt Minh. Alone to take care of her family in Huế, Cam became a 'single' mom.

By this time, after six years of marriage, grandma Cam already had her own house, her own growing family, two daughters and a son. To make it even harder, she was in the second trimester. Finding herself in need of support in time of chaos, Cam moved back in with her parents in the big old house where she'd grown up. The fighting continued. Cam pulled up her sleeves and contributed to the household. She would carry goods she bought in Huế to sell them to merchants in Quảng Trị and Đà Nẵng. Quảng Trị is 32 miles northwest of Huế, and Đà Nẵng 49 miles southeast of Huế. The round-trip to each place would take up to a month. When on the road, grandma would leave her three children in the care of the adults of the big family. After a few trips, Cam realized that she did not make enough to provide adequately for her children. She did not want to depend on her siblings.

One day, an acquaintance told her that, if she was unable to raise all her children, she could send one of her daughters to the Catholic convent where the nuns helped take care of the children. It was common at the time for 'single' mothers in grandma Cam's situation to send their daughters to the nunnery for a short period. In fact, my grandmother Quyên, my father's mom, with her husband away with the Việt Minh after 1946 and herself overwhelmed with four children, did send one of her daughters to stay in a Catholic convent for a year before getting her back. But grandma

Cam rejected the idea outright. Instead, she looked for a way to get her family back together with her husband.

After two years without hearing anything from grandfather, in 1948, grandma Cam managed to connect with the revolutionary force. She prepared to move her family to where her husband was. She first made the trip herself to Bình Định to see with her own eyes life in the liberated zone. Now that she knew what to expect on the road and in the new land, she made a second trip, this time taking all her three children.

They started the journey from Huế to Bình Định at the end of 1949. Grandma Cam sold her house in Huế for a low price to have some money under her belt. Aunt Hương was eight, my mom seven, my uncle four. As the youngest, and probably skinny and light as a feather, uncle Tuấn was carried in a basket hanging on one side of the pole held by a helper grandma hired. In the other basket, there were clothes and food supplies for the whole family. Together with one or two other families, and a guide who probably worked for the Việt Minh, grandma started the journey at nightfall.

Going south, the road from Huế to Bình Định is approximately 263 miles. "To keep a low profile, everyone traveled on foot for most of the trip," aunt Hương narrated. "The French soldiers were searching the roads intensively for the Việt Minh. A sign of people on the road meant bombings followed; therefore most of the time we hid during the day and walked at night."

By this time, I was deep in the stories. I did not notice before but it is very quiet inside a house in Đà Lạt. To keep the warmth we close all doors and windows. We could hear quietness the moment we stopped talking. I was concerned the silence made aunt Hương uncomfortable. She was not. She smiled more often as she went along, and she laughed in short bursts here and there. Her voice began to level out keeping pace. *It would be a long story.* I relaxed my tense muscles, eased up in the chair, and stretched my imagination with full joy. Revisiting her eight-year-old self was nothing but one intimate moment aunt Hương had with the dearest memory of her mom. She enjoyed telling me grandma stories and appreciated my attentive ears.

I imagined the topography of the regions they passed to be diverse and tempestuous as the feelings and anxiety in the heart and mind of all members of the group. In secret, they shared their hopes and dreams. In silence, they walked the roads. When it was raining, dirt roads became a nightmare, so much so that one could almost feel how water soaked the kids' souls and chilled them to ice.

"On such an occasion, the dirt path under our feet was slippery, wet darkness over our head, danger in the back, and hell in front of us," my mom described in her unpublished memoir, "the miserable refugees treaded on." Children and adults were squabbling in darkness. Suddenly, Cam felt the tugging on her back and heard her daughter's frightening whisper: "I cannot see the road, *Má*. I am so scared." That little girl's voice is my mom recalling. Cam, unable to offer a hand as both were full of stuff already, told her daughter: "Grab my blouse and walk, *con*."

"Some other times, we crossed the river by boat," aunt Hương told me. "It must have been an important river because the French searched it thoroughly. If they heard a noise on the river, they responded with gun fire in return. The group sat in the tiny boat quietly, not daring to move a muscle. Even breathing was a serious task to tend to. We were instructed to breathe lightly enough so only we could hear ourselves.

"After a few days, the guide informed us that it was alright to walk during the day now. At the crack of dawn, we started walking. From morning to afternoon we walked. At the sound of the helicopter, everyone stooped down in the rice field pressing their chest and even their face as close to the murky gooey water as possible. We waited. After things went quiet, we rose back up, wet and dirty from head to toe."

When not in hiding, standing up under the scorching sun was not a pleasant thing, either, as the heat seemed to burn up any liquid they had left in their bodies. My mom remembered my grandma

Cam giving the children a handful of young tea leaves and told them to put one in their mouth and suck it to keep them hydrated.

At times when they were passing rice paddies that spread till they met the skyline, my mom recounted, the group guide reached out and picked a few stems of rice plant on top of which bundles of tiny young rice grains were bulging up waiting to ripe. He put the cluster of green rice bulbs in his mouth and sucked them. Others in the group imitated. Inside the tiny rice bulbs, drops of milky and sweet liquid burst in their mouth. This magnificent gift from the land saved the weary passengers from the deadly thirst.

In the evening, they reached some shelter for their much-needed rest of the day.

"Not all the threat came from the enemy or the elements," my mom said.

"One day the group stopped at the foot of a mountain to prepare to climb a pass. It could be Hải Vân pass. It is too long ago and I was too young to tell. But I guessed so because it is the one major mountain we had to climb before we reached Quảng Ngãi and then Bình Định. Hải Vân pass was known to be populated by tigers. It was good common sense to pass during the day and not at night, so the group put up make-shift bamboo shelters and gathered around.

"It was hot in the jungle. Surrounded by tremendous space, people in the group still did not know where to go and what to do to shake off the weariness that clung to them from the long and arduous journey.

"Out of the blue, somebody sang:

> *Climbing up Chuối mountain at mid-day,*
> *Why do you look so somber, mountain? I asked*
> *I feel sorry for you humans, she replied,*
> *Who have to leave your mother and father behind*
>   *for a soldier's life.*

"A young man in the group kept reciting the same lines many times over. The melancholy in his voice only added bleakness to the situation amplified through the jungle by the heavy air. It stuck in my head to this day."

At nightfall, they built a fire. Nobody dared to venture far from the shelter.

Suddenly grandma Cam cried out in fright: "Where is my son? *Con ơi!*"

People looked around and it was true my uncle Tuấn was gone. Everybody rushed out of the shelter in all directions to go look for him. They had to find him before the tigers might. They went as far as where they thought the four-year-old could have gone. There was no sight of him. Grandma began to tear up. Then suddenly somebody found him squatting in the thick bush near the shelter. The boy said to grandma Cam: "I was fighting with my friend and I was afraid you would scold me so I went hiding in the bush!" Grandma Cam cried with relief and gave her son a bear hug.

Once a while, they stopped by a creek. Adults came together, cooked rice and prepared dinner while children wandered around playing with water. This was one moment of peace and relaxation during the strenuous trip that aunt Hương recalled. It replenished in everybody the promise of freedom in the liberated zone to which they were heading.

Still some other days, they found themselves on top of a hill thickly filled with bamboo trees. And they continued to walk. One month, or two months, or longer passed—aunt Hương was too young to count precisely—and they reached their destination, a small town in the South Central coastal region of Bình Định province, Bồng Sơn, where my grandfather worked. It was early 1950.

* * *

I was shocked out of my lucid mind to find out that my grandmother Quyên, my dad's mother, also made this same trip, around the same time, though not in the same group, from Huế to Bình

Định to find her husband. Unlike grandmother Cam, grandma Quyên left her four children behind with her siblings and went on the trip by herself. She later made the trip back to Huế with her husband instead of staying in Bình Định like grandma Cam. The main point remains that both grandmas Quyên and Cam walked in secret for many weeks hiding from the French soldiers covering 263 miles, between Huế and Bình Định, to search for their husbands.

Why grandmas were the ones who had to go look for grandpas, I don't understand. It is more logical for grandpas to go to their families when the time was right—each having a wife and three to four children waiting for them—and especially given that grandma Cam had to make two trips to get everyone together. Everybody I asked, aunts and uncles, relatives close and far, told me: "It is how things went at the time." As if there was no other choice. As if men of the time, particularly educated ones, were not supposed to lift any finger.

"I know that is how things went at the time but it does not make it a logical or a right thing," I told them. "You have to stop defending the outdated traditions and start criticizing them because that is the only way for change to happen."

"But that is how things went at the time," came their response. They did not get it. There is always a huge 'but' in their refrain, so big it blindsides them all. I got more frustrated.

"For your grandfather to move from liberated Bồng Sơn to Huế would mean risking living in hiding for a long time, as many did," my mother explained. "As a civil servant working for the Việt Minh, grandfather Tín could travel with relative ease in the free zones as long as he had official business. The moment he entered the French-patrolled areas, without proper documentation, he would be in big trouble. And Huế was back under French control in 1946. To the French, he was a Việt Minh they were hunting, even though he used to work for the French. In case he could not stay in Huế and had to go back to Bồng Sơn, this very tricky and diabolical situation made him look, in the Việt Minh's eyes, as a defector they could never trust. Eventually, nobody from either side could trust him. That is why grandfather was stuck in Bình Định."

I accepted some facts in her response. Yet, that explanation reveals that Vietnamese people tend to jump quickly, as a reflex, at defending the wrong-doer, e.g. the man, instead of expressing sympathy and understanding for the victim, e.g. the woman. Their reasoning also shows that people still do not seem to be bothered at all by the fact that Vietnamese women are the ones who take all the actions, and they are taken for granted!

Deep down I want to believe that there always is a choice. When left alone to take care of her four children without a husband, grandma Quyên, also the daughter of a mandarin, made a heart-breaking decision to send her oldest daughter to live with her aunt, Quyên's sister, in a convent for a year. She also had to send her 6-year-old son, my father, to live with his uncle in a different city for a year, so that she could better care for the other two. And most importantly, so that all four of her children could go to school without interruption. Grandma Quyên was also an intelligent woman who had to cut short her education at the end of fourth grade to help her mom around the house. She promised herself to secure the best education for all her children. So if you think that in wartime and chaos people only have the mind to survive and nobody would care about education, think again! On that matter, grandma Cam held the same belief. She chose to send her kids away for the best education possible. She decided to take her children to reunite with her husband only on the second trip for safety concerns. All those cataclysmic events that my grandmas pulled through involve near-impossible decisions that they made to protect the family and for the sake of their children's well-being. Every single one required courage, astuteness, absolute love and wisdom to follow through. Grandma Cam and grandma Quyên understood well the risks and the possible loss involved in each situation, and they made their choices clear. They are as strong as the toughest man I have ever known. Even stronger. It is childish and old-fashioned to believe that only muscles can move mountains. My grandmas had their own visions of life. And they aimed for the best.

* * *

The other day I came across a few pictures a friend in Vietnam posted on his Facebook wall after one of his trips home to visit family in the countryside. In one, four women and a man, aged between twenty and thirty, are gathered around an old woman. Everyone is smiling happily and toothily. There is obvious energy, enthusiasm, and a sense of satisfaction on the faces of the young people. *They must have good jobs and love what they are doing.* The lady's peppered hair tied back in a bun. She is wearing a short-sleeved blouse, collar-less, buttoned-front, and probably loose pants, a typical *đồ bà ba* daily wear for people in the countryside fit for the tropical weather and humidity in Vietnam. The subdued pattern and earth tone color of the outfit say as much. Above their head in the background, I saw tin roof, and right underneath it a few cardboard boxes are held together by two long wooden sticks anchoring themselves on top of a high wall on one side and a beam on the other. The two horizontal wooden sticks have thin combs between them so that the small boxes would not fall through. It is a simple temporary-looking hand-crafted shelf, indication of a modest house.

The other picture is more panoramic and with even more gleeful faces. The elderly woman is now standing inside the room right at the open door. Seven young women and a young man cheer around her, everyone smiling, everyone showing their teeth, including the center lady—she really smiled. The freckled skin added age to her round face without hiding the positivity oozing from her eyes and the once youthfulness and beauty that still shine. Kindness, wisdom and strength I perceived in her. She shrinks, with aging. The girls on the right and left embrace her affectionately over her shoulder and belly. These young women, in tight jeans, sleeveless or open neck T-shirts, or bright colorful shirts, are a head or two taller than her. They bend down at her height, leaning on each other's shoulder, crossing arms like a band marching in camaraderie. Outside the door, the afternoon sun tilts over the garden dazzling out the rest of the landscape.

On the space where we are supposed to answer Facebook's stimulating question "What's on your mind today?" a caption to the pictures reads: "My mom in her kitchen..." Not: "My mom and the youngsters..." Or: "My mom and my ladies..." Or even: "My mom in the kitchen..." *Her* kitchen! I could not believe my eyes. On seeing the word *her kitchen* I felt a choke rising up my throat.

I know the author meant to honor his mom. By specifically declaring her the sole owner of the kitchen he made her a boss—an honor, indeed. In an almost bulletproof message that combined the fireproof elements of mother and an indication of food initiating cozy images and emotions, to generate the most likes. After all, in a hierarchical society such as Vietnam each one of us has a headful of engraved images about what our mother is supposed to be. Rarely does anyone question these deposits. Embedded in this ore lies the consistent association of 'mom' to 'kitchen' which we normally perceive as comforting, and the familiar perceptions of her as weak, resigned to fate and submissive—all the misconceptions I learned when small in books and in life around me that I now wish to dispel. If mom imparts in you wisdom and strength, teaches you financial maturity, and encourages you to build a strong character and pursue your dreams, as she definitely does from the way my friend shows off his mom glowing in her kitchen like a goddess, she is more than a kitchen goddess.

Young professionals, high achievers in Vietnam these days, talk openly about their humble background, to highlight a contrast to their polished presence and make it appear larger and shinier. It is a testimony to their confidence, and a laureate to their current success. I hail this action. The ubiquity of social media only adds to the volume of their buzzing messages. One would think that, to match their 'new' status, it makes more sense for the youngsters to stay away from the cozy, familiar, worn out, non-creative and erroneous efforts of celebrating mom in the kitchen, an association that only screams status quo, stagnancy, hypocrisy.

Only if it works that way.

I know too well that, to this day, many Vietnamese people still interpret their mom's or grandma's sadness, sorrow, or gentleness as a sign of submissiveness, and a resignation to fate. Women in my mom's generation went to school and got an education. Most made a career for themselves. But education or not, career or not, everyone worked and took care of their family. In return, they are not talked about directly as submissive or resigned to fate; they are politely and lovingly adored in their kitchen. If a mom or a grandmother is, fortunately, blessed with a constant smile, she does so in her kitchen. As if the kids are saying: *I love you, Mom, but your place is still in the corner.* I have never seen a picture of a dad captioned: "My dad in his kitchen!" The general perception and expectation of Vietnamese women in society is pretty much unchanged—a damsel in distress, she has to wait to be rescued in her kitchen. No wonder the 'reputation' spreads outside Vietnamese borders and Vietnamese women are presumed as such.

I did not buy into this kind of thinking, and never will. Both grandma Quyên and grandma Cam found their own ways in life, especially after marriage, like other Vietnamese women. It is their resilience, strength, and wisdom that have sustained the generations of Vietnamese people. This, I would not let others tell me otherwise.

Even as a kid, before I could formulate my own thoughts, I always felt the simmering fighting souls of the Vietnamese women around me. I have carried their sadness and sorrow in my mind with an obsession to purge them not only from myself but from Vietnamese mentality. My grandma Quyên and grandma Cam are those who absorb in their veins a purely vernacular Vietnamese culture. Embellished, romantic or poetic expressions of emotions are strangers in their everyday vocabulary. By not being used to vocalizing their fighting and demands publicly, they leave space for the exotic interpretation of their character and risk being marked 'submissive.' Make no mistake, deep beyond the non-vocalized deeds, the simplicity in their heart's desire for happiness together with honesty in their no-makeup personality have woven the thread of sobriety in Vietnamese life. *And I inherited that thread.* The psychological pressure of their assumed pent-up emotions, that could have crushed their spirit as expected in Western thinking, is canceled out by the reality and demands of running an every-day family life with efficiency, *and* an unflinching hope for a better future.

Grandma Cam did not have the liberty to marry out of love, but her belief in love is running in my veins. Her sacrifice to secure her children's education and happiness etched in my mind. As I listened to her stories, I felt her pain, I felt her yearning for freedom, I felt her life.

I chose love, passion, and happiness at an early age before I could even define what they meant. They were urges inside of me unexplainable yet indispensable. They grew in me and I nurtured them. Until one day, with a light heart and a lucid mind, I was strong enough to forge a path in life for myself.

3. HOW

"HOW DID YOU GET TO the U.S.?" they would ask me.

"I received a scholarship to come here," I always told them.

"Are you a party member? Or do you have any connection to the communist government?"

"No," I said. And I saw disbelief in their eyes.

I have met a lot of Vietnamese Americans. The conversation above was one of the most common between us the first few years after I arrived. Every time, I stressed the fact that I was not a party member or anything similar, that I was awarded the scholarship to come here to study. But they didn't seem to believe it. At first, I was baffled at why white Americans believed me but not Vietnamese Americans. Which part of the story induced disbelief in the latter, I did not know. After a few encounters it struck me that, for most boat people who left Vietnam in the 70s or 80s, their memory of the country stopped at the moment of their leaving. Their amnesia is the result of a decade of isolation and non-communication between Vietnam and most of the rest of the world after the war ended in 1975. There was hardly news of relatives or family they left behind. The emotional distance that ensued only enhanced the nostalgia and longing that formed, freezing an ocean-sized wound in their miserable souls. They have carried this pain and the frozen image of home. According to this memory frame, Vietnamese people lived under the tight control of the communist party and government. People could hardly move around, in or out of where they were. Young Vietnamese could only nurture a hope for studying abroad if their family had close ties with the party or the right kind of connections. These were once facts.

But things changed a lot at the turn of the century. Vietnam re-established diplomatic relations with the U.S. in 1995 and American corporations began to flock back. The country was already well on track to capitalism purely in terms of economy. Economic growth and development released pressure on other aspects of life. Traveling and moving around for work have become commonplace. Everyone can apply for a passport and get out of the country with a proper visa. The Vietnamese government does not care to stop them from leaving anymore. The paperwork is still a nuisance, but a ticket out is possible.

I told them that too. They listened quietly and gave no response, as if unwilling to accept that some measure of freedom exists in a 'capitalist-slash-communist' Vietnam. They averted their eyes. The look of puzzlement remained, as if I was telling them fictions to make myself look good. As if everybody is hiding something.

I understood the power of denial and skepticism and did not try to reason with them.

* * *

I was teaching ESL as a lecturer at the then University of Hồ Chí Minh city.

One very hot day in Spring, I finished teaching and went to the chairwoman's office to see my friend who was the secretary to the Chair. After we chatted, I sat down on the long couch, pulled out a pile of papers and started to grade. I had never hung out in the Chairwoman's office like this before. Even now thinking back I still have no idea why I wanted to do so on that day. It must have been the raging heat outside that quelled my habitual behavior as an abiding citizen.

Ten minutes later, the Chairwoman returned. As she sat down at her desk and began to go through the pile of documents in front of her, I wrapped up the papers and prepared to leave. Suddenly, I heard her say: "There is a scholarship from some Brigham Young University. It is a masters degree program in American Studies for one person." Then she paused. I ignored what I heard.

I was looking for a scholarship to study abroad at the time, like thousands of other young Vietnamese, with no plan to go through a government channel though. At the university then, and in all institutions around the country, everybody knew seniority came first. (It still does.) As long as I worked for a public institution, I learned to follow the rules of the game. We all did. I had been teaching for only five years. There were many others who taught there for ten years or more and their turn to be selected to apply for a scholarship would come before mine. Not believing in waiting, I focused on direct communications with the U.S. universities. Confident in the ultimate fairness of the American system (I was very naive then), I believed I would get a scholarship in the near future. So I paid no attention to the news.

Suddenly, I heard the chairwoman say my name.

"Anvi, why don't you apply for it? I will also ask Ng. to apply as well."

Or maybe, at some point Ng., who had a few years my seniority, entered the room and the chairwoman asked him to apply. Then she turned to me and asked me to do the same. I don't remember which scenario. Either way, I remembered being shocked to hear my name called. *She was just being nice.* Trying to play my part, I said: "Oh no. I am sure others with more seniority would be happy to apply." Showing respect to your seniors was, and still is, the norm.

To my surprise, she insisted that I apply for the scholarship. "You should apply. You and Ng., you two are young and enthusiastic. You two do it. The application deadline is in two days."

"Are you serious about asking me to apply?" I asked with suspicion in my voice and probably my face as well, still thinking she was messing with my head. She repeated: "Yes!" My friend also chimed in and encouraged me to take the offer from the Chair.

"If you say so," I told the chairwoman, "I will apply."

On the drive home, I could not get the excitement, the confusion and the expediency of the situation out of my head. I thought the only reason she asked me to apply was because no one had heard of BYU before, and the department had no relationship with it whatsoever, which meant the scholarship might not pan out. Back then we relied on scholarships from the Ford Foundation, a sister university or institution we already had relations with, which meant the offers would be for real. After many years seeing how things worked, people believed that was the only way to go abroad for higher education. I was not surprised that BYU, as an unfamiliar name, raised doubt about its legitimacy and probability. Besides, the deadline was in two days. It did sound like a cruel joke.

Joke or not, I had nothing to lose by trying. I was totally prepared. My months-old TOEFL test score was very high, exceeding the requirement for any U.S. university; I had a 15-page paper to use as a writing sample. At the time when the longest term paper we were required to write in college was three pages, my sample should be totally impressive. I could furnish a statement of purpose in a couple of hours.

I submitted my application on the due date.

Ten years later I learned that many of my colleagues were asked to apply for BYU at the time. Most of them refused to do it. They did not believe in it, or they did not have time to gather the application materials. I had no clue why they said no to such an opportunity. In the end, only two of us applied and went through the processes. After two rounds of in-person interviews, I received news that I would go to BYU in Provo, Utah, to join the masters program in American Studies.

That is the story of how I got to the U.S. I don't think the Vietnamese Americans believe this one, either. Again, it is the power of denial.

4. LOGIC

I ARRIVED IN THE UNITED STATES on June twenty-ninth of 2001 at Denver airport. Before the trip I had already heard things about the U.S. and it sounded exhilarating. Just as everybody in Vietnam already knew: America is paradise, a land of opportunities. So I worked up my excitement as the plane got nearer to destination. I paid attention to my feelings and was waiting for some magical moment to happen.

It was a few months before 9/11, therefore, I could say with honor and confidence that I did experience, in many ways, what I called 'the original American dream' that I'd heard so much about. No security whatsoever at the airport, and people came and went as if at a market! My cousins and their families were waiting at the arrival gate. I got off the plane, walked through the conduit, and they were right there standing and smiling at me.

It was an exciting moment, my aunt hugged me, I greeted others, and we chatted our way to the baggage claim area. I knew I had to be on the alert about everything around me to record my original reactions to the new land, but it was difficult to do it when so much talking and different kinds of noise and movements were going on.

I had not seen my cousins for a long time. We used to live next door in Vietnam. After ten years, they had not changed much. Some gained a little bit of weight. Cousin Trâm was still skinny and quiet. And of course I could not help noticing that the airport was so clean and shining. There were restaurants with names I had not seen before. Shops with glittering displays. At some point I was sur-prised by the honking. *Why honking in the airport.* I turned around and saw the airport cart wheezing through. Some older people were on it. *That is good thinking,* a thought popped in my head, *to help older citizens.* I heard a public announcement about some flight. People were pulling their luggage and walking past me. They were very quick. Most of them were in a hurry, I guessed. Or they were just faster than me because they were bigger and taller. Or both. Many people were sitting and waiting on the benches in front of the gates. All these tall and big Americans around me. Just a glimpse, I could not detect any kind of emotion. But they appeared friendly. I did not face any threatening look that made me feel I was being judged in any way. Around me, there was a lot of space and a ton of things and people.

Down at the carousels, suitcases were spit out of an opening and fell onto the moving steel conveyor. In 2001, flying in Vietnam was not at all a popular means of transportation as it is today, and very expensive. I was used to express buses, speedboats and trains. This was actually the first time I had flown. At the Singapore airport during transfer, I kept touching the gigantic and vibrant orchid plants unconvinced they were real. Everything during the trip was new and exciting to me, especially when my first baggage claim experience happened in the U.S. I could not help poking my eyes into everything. I was obsessed about exploring the new things and confirming the familiar assumptions, because I, learning from Sherlock Holmes when small, believe that everything connects and every detail yields clues.

Later in the U.S., I read that Einstein said the same thing: ev-erything connects. I don't know who was the first to say this. It could go back as far as the Hellenistic period. So, at the luggage area, I inspected everything. I walked around the conveyer belt and saw the sign: "No siting on moving belt." *It makes sense.* Lots of people were waiting around the conveyor. Everybody stayed calm and waited for their luggage. Once they snatched it off the belt, they checked the label, then pulled it along and disappeared from the crowd. It was an efficient operation. I was not surprised at this orderly behavior. I expected it, actually, from the civilized society I assumed America was. As the belt was moving around, the shining blades of metal expanding and contracting caught my attention. I wondered whether something was ever caught between these blades. And how they made sure that did not happen. *Maybe these blades are accident-proof. It is the U.S., after all.* Efficiency was the first thing about America that impressed me. I did not consider this my first impression of America, though. I was expecting something magical.

I kept watch of my thoughts vigorously like a dog protecting her newborns. Within fifteen or twenty minutes I already felt overwhelmed at my own expectations and the task I set for myself in facing the new world I was about to explore in the years to come. *There is no way I could record and take note of everything around me. There is simply too much information to process.*

On the way out, in the noise and with exhaustion, I remembered vaguely something special about the white floating roof of this airport. After that we reached the garage and got in a big van. As the van started moving, I panicked thinking that my first few minutes in America were coming to an end and nothing had happened yet. I tried to open my eyes wide waiting to see myself get a culture shock. I had imagined my first impression of America to be something shocking and was waiting for that to happen.

The van got out of the airport and into the highway. Arid field after field outside the airport—that was what I saw. The roads were very big with multiple lanes, and so clean. There were a lot of cars. Actually, there were only cars and no motorcycle or bicycle or pedestrian traffic whatsoever on the road. I had heard this about the U.S. while still in Vietnam. Cement, iron, steel, rock—it felt industrial and efficient to me. People drove fast. It was an easy drive.

After twenty minutes I was disappointed at myself for not jumping up and down at spectacles on the sides of the road. My heart did not tinkle with surprises. *This could not be my first impression of America*, I thought and began to feel panic again. *There had to be something that I may have already missed.* For a second, I felt regret for not being attentive enough to register all my reactions. Too worried I could not go back to recreate my first impression.

Years later, I wondered whether I would have felt differently had I arrived at night and on the drive past the big city I had seen the skyline from afar. Would I have been thrilled at the sight of the skyscrapers and neon lights mapping the city against the dark horizon? Maybe not. Maybe because I had so much of that in Hollywood movies, reality could no longer surprise me. Or to me, America was more of an abstract idea rather than the physical attraction of materials I heard so many people talking about. In any case, for the rest of the drive to my aunt's house in Aurora, I found myself thinking a lot. I made my brain work hard in the name of 'my first impression of America.' The harder I tried the more confusing and tiring I became.

Less than an hour later, the van got off the freeway and entered residential roads into a quiet neighborhood. The front yard of the houses that we passed seemed to share the same pattern of grey from the roof and green from the lawn and the evergreen. We stopped in front of a two-story modest-looking house. My aunt's front yard stood out a bit more with many colorful flowers. This I also heard in Vietnam when my cousins came back and told us that American soil was very good and that Vietnamese people tended to plant a lot of flowers around the house to make it look nice.

Once inside, it was much more spacious than I imagined: three bedrooms and two baths upstairs; two more bedrooms, a bath, and a huge family room in the walk-out basement. The main floor contained the living-room, the kitchen, another family room and the dining quarter. My aunt was pretty sick at the time waiting to have a liver transplant that could happen any moment. Because of her health condition, my cousins turned the living room into her living quarter so that she did not have to walk around that much. Her husband also stayed there, nearby to tend to all her needs.

In general, not counting the modification to accommodate my aunt, I was impressed with the clear-cut assignment of space use in the design of an American house. Very different from a typical thin tall multi-function multi-level vertical house in Sài Gòn I was familiar with. This type of house is disappearing in Vietnam in the twenty-first century. A big city is a copycat of a European or metropolitan American one. High-end interior design and building materials are imports from around the world. A lesser version of the Western model is littering the countryside. A multi-level house now can simple serve a single family, not an extended one. The traditional world I knew will be extinct soon.

I went to the upstairs room reserved for me, unpacked some clothes and gifts, and we began days of celebration with food, drink and talking.

My aunt, An, and her family had settled in America in the early 1990s. During the 'Vietnam War,' her husband, Vinh, was a Major in the South Vietnam Army. In 1975 when the war ended, he was sent to a re-education camp for fifteen years. By this time, the U.S. government had rolled out the Humanitarian Operation (HO) program that aimed to help with U.S. immigration for South Vietnamese people who were involved in the old regime or worked for the U.S. and suffered communist persecution after 1975. Uncle Vinh and his family fit the category perfectly. They applied to the HO program. Within a year they immigrated to America and started a new life. By this time, two of their oldest daughters and their families had already settled down in America. They came earlier also as HO immigrants based on their husbands' status. When the big family arrived, they helped them ease into the new life.

My uncle Đinh, my dad's younger brother, who was a pilot in the South Vietnam Air Force and who spent seven years in the re-education camp, also registered for the HO program and moved to America a couple of years following my aunt's family. He also lived in Aurora, ten minutes away from my aunt. Uncle Đinh arranged for me to stay with my aunt and her family. "It's more fun over there," he said. "Over here, it's only a four-person household including my two grown-up children. It would be quiet and lonely for you." Besides, aunt An was older. She got the final word about my staying at her place and there was no argument about that.

My aunt An had nine children, five daughters and four sons. One son with his family remained in Vietnam. Of the eight in the U.S., one son lived with his family in Southern California, three other married daughters and their families resided minutes away from her, and the three singles stayed at home with her. A newly wed son and his wife also lived here because it was a big house. They wanted to save some money to buy their own house later. They also wanted to help chip in with the mortgage. On top of that, they could help take care of his mom. This couple moved to another city when the son got a new job as a software engineer.

For the moment, the house was like a non-stop operation. There was always some food on the long dining table in the kitchen. Somebody would be going in and out of the house at all times. Two of my single cousins worked two different shifts at the post office. The other single guy was out all the time and back at odd hours—I hardly saw him. I did not even know where he worked—I heard banking or finance or something like that. Uncle Vinh, my aunt's husband, also had an on-the-move bug. When my aunt was stable without needing his support, meetings with old comrades or fishing trips kept him busy. I did not see him a lot, either, except on the days he was around to help my aunt babysit their baby granddaughter. Meanwhile, the nearby daughters and the in-laws would often drop by after work, if not daily, sometimes with their children, just to have a word with their mom—my aunt; to taste some food; to pick up the sweater they left behind; to bring over some delicacies for their parents and grandparents; to pick up the baby, for one couple; et cetera, et cetera. There was no need to call in advance before coming over. As a clan leader, my aunt provided around-the-clock support to everybody. She also manned the headquarter here where all kinds of news relating to everybody circulated, including from Vietnam.

Then during the weekend, all the grandchildren ranging in age from six months to twelve years old would come. The house became a county fair. Baby crying and laughing, everybody talking, children running, teenagers teasing and screaming, more baby laughing. But mostly talking and laughing filled the air already infused with food fragrance. My aunt would happily be hard at work in the kitchen all day long. In spite of the pain she suffered, she tried to move around as much as she could. "I could not stand lying on my back all day long," she said.

It was like I got out of Vietnam to come back *home* here in Aurora, Colorado. No wonder many Vietnamese Americans think that it is here in the U.S. that we preserve the essence of Vietnamese culture, not in Vietnam where many strongly believe the battle between traditions and modernity is already lost and the country is speedily falling apart at the seams. I had yet to form an opinion on that. Observation and listening were all I did.

Aunt An was my favorite. Very clever and with an incredible sense of humor. She was the center of the conversation and an endless source of entertainment, especially when she impersonated other people. Frowning and twisting her voice, sometimes coupled with hand and body movements, she cracked everybody up. A dinner party became less exciting without her.

Aunt An came to the U.S. in her mid sixties speaking very little English. She said with regret once: "I wish I spoke more English and understood the language better." Across from her kitchen was the big screen television. She would have it on all the time to watch news. In spite of her limited English, aunt An kept herself very much updated with current affairs. She would know what President Bush was doing; be aware of news, discoveries and events around the world; keep up with the weather and accidents around the country, with new commercialized gadgets, as well as celebrity gossips. These were the things she talked about, not just her children and grandchildren. She would ask questions frequently, when somebody was around, about things she saw on TV that she could not decipher.

When I was in Aurora, I hung out in the kitchen with her and we talked. Sometimes, many hours during the day, there was only aunt An and me at home. She was always cooking something, for the weekend, for cousins Trâm and Trang to pack lunch, or for frozen put-away. She did not need a reason to cook. With so many children and grandchildren around, no amount of food was enough for her.

I helped her prep. It reminded me of when I was small and hung around like a shadow to watch her work. Between my mom and her, I mastered the sous chef skills from those observation sessions—I was very handy and became her favorite niece because of that. I was second only to her when it comes to slicing, chopping, peeling, dicing, shredding, carving, rolling, kneading, and anything else in between. It was fun now to work with the master again.

However, right now, thoughts about the new school occupied me. I planned to visit them a week then head off to Brigham Young University to prepare for school. I greatly appreciated the time here in Aurora with my aunt and her family but did not enjoy cooking or doing dishes at all. Resisting them may be too strong a word to describe how I felt. I understand housework is the major contribution to the family my aunt could do at this stage in her life, in the new homeland, and she did an extraordinary job. This achievement inadvertently invokes in me the old familiar association of women to the kitchen making my whole experience in the U.S. too Vietnamese to make any sense. A part of me could not help but cringe in fear. As if a longer stay with my cousins would make me become too Vietnamese to adjust to the new American environment. As if the moment I entered America I was Westernized; turning Vietnamese was a backward step. I was afraid the Vietnamese atmosphere could stain my new Western aura.

Soon I began to feel restless.

In the meantime, with so many sounds and activities going on around the house, all the food and gatherings, and all the catching up and visits to do, I forgot about my 'real' first impression of

America. Even though I somehow expected, as a taciturn person, my first reaction to setting foot on the U.S. soil to be lukewarm, but also because of all the hype I heard and read about the States, I quickly developed an urge to mold my first impression of America to be crystal clear in my mind. I wanted it to be something I could tell, or better impress, others when asked. At the moment, it was not clear. But it was there like a nagging presence. I felt it the whole time I stayed in Aurora.

After a few days of feasts and proper resting, it became clear in my mind and stuck with me until now: the street signs in Colorado—they were perfect.

During the drive from the airport to the Aurora house, I was on the bench right behind the driver, my cousin Định, occupying the middle space where my sight was not obstructed by either the driver or the front-seat passenger, my other cousin Mai. Leaning forward to look at the road ahead, I followed the signs as Định was driving. Interspersed in their talk about family and life in America were their comments about directions. I noticed that the instructions on the boards were very clear, easy to understand and follow. Indications of what was about to happen the next mile or two, how far the coming cities were, etc. helped a great deal to prepare the driver. *What a clever system it is!* I could not help thinking.

This very fascination with the road signs soon gave way to the festivities at the house. When I got my full senses back, it dawned on me that if you could design traffic signs that everybody, such as a foreigner like me coming to the U.S. for the first time, could understand without a mistake like that, you were a genius, if not somebody with impeccable logical thinking already. Then I thought, logic is a promising door to it all. Good logic led to efficiency and science and productivity, and so on. *No wonder America is a great country!* I concluded. American logic was a very reasonable way of thinking that made living and working here pleasant. The type of reasoning that oiled the whole system and enabled dreams to spurt. Exactly what I wanted to see in America.

What I did not know at the time is that this logic is not un-changing from state to state and in the whole country over time. It is difficult to defend it now and then when news of police shooting black people or a mass shooting at the mall explodes across the TV screen every week or so. And the intense debates on immigration issues render real fear into colored people's lives.

Yet, back then, that logic story was about the first dot—second, actually, to efficiency—of reality I could connect to the image of America I had in mind. I decided it was magnificent enough to be remembered as my real first impression of America—something I was proud to tell when asked.

* * *

I stayed in Aurora past July 4. It was hot but I don't remember much about the heat, except that my uncle Vinh and my cousin Trâm kept watering the garden. It is normally one hundred percent humidity in Vietnam. If anything, the dry heat of Aurora made it more comfortable and bearable for me.

I spent several days going to places with my cousins for fun, including a camping trip by the lake. They said it was not very far, less than two hours away. "And you call that 'not very far'?" I rolled my eyes. They said casually: "Yes."

I did the calculation in my head. About a hundred miles meant twice the distance between Sài Gòn and the beach city of Vũng Tàu in the south. When I was growing up, when traveling and trans-portation were limited, when Vũng Tàu was the vacation place for those of us from Sài Gòn and further who wished to get there once a year, it was a l-o-n-g distance. We would wake up at four or five in the morning to get ready and go to the meeting point, then it took us three to four hours to get to the beach.

Here, for a hundred miles, we just packed and went. Wow. *I need to get used to the concept of distance here in the U.S.. So many things to learn.*

Young Vietnamese living in a big city these days deal with dis-tance in a similar way Americans do, now that owning a car is a common thing in Vietnam. From Sài Gòn, they often pack and go to Vũng Tàu for a day trip or the weekend.

A bunch of us fit into a minivan and another car. We got to the lake around mid afternoon. It would be dark in a few hours. Some of us set up the tents. Others built a campfire and prepared dinner. After dinner, we crawled into the tent and went to sleep. We would go hiking the next day.

I woke up early next morning. Got out of the tent and the misty blue lake was right there. It was breath-taking. I could not take my eyes off of it. A swan was swimming leisurely. The fog was trying to linger around just a little bit longer but it was receding gradually because the sun was up. The crisp air, blue sky, blue water and shining sun seemed to enhance my senses. Suddenly, my increasing appreciation for the organization of life in America sunk in. There is work, and play, and social activities. You work hard, you play hard, you maintain social involvement. And you don't mix them together. It is a compartmentalized mentality I saw reflected in the design of an American house. Totally in contrast to the multi-level multi-function house in Vietnam which mirrors a fusion sensibility that I had. There was no talk whatsoever about concepts of work, play, and social life when I was growing up. There was only a tough life and how to survive it.

Standing now by the blue lake, I gained a new perspective which made me believe at the time that American life *was* the other way of living that I was looking for. I felt the enjoyment in people who appeared content and happy with the opportunity to pursue a lifestyle of their choice in America. It showed on their faces, in their voices, and behaviors. Optimism and a sense of hope were visible everywhere.

I walked on the dirt path full of little rocks and edged near the lake. Many campers were also up. They dotted around the lake taking pictures. In the cool air, in the middle of the woods, more alert than ever, I felt the sense of freedom that propelled so many people all over the world to willingly make sacrifices at all cost, even risking their lives, to get here. I was breathing that air of freedom right now.

I simply stood staring at the lake, shocked by the pristine nature surrounding me.

* * *

The last few days of my stay, my cousins took me shopping. Every store we stopped by was gigantic: Goodwill, Dillard's, Ross. In each place, I found myself presented with way too many choices. So many pants, so many tops, so many jackets and dresses, and they were in all styles and colors, and so much more. Being used to the tropical weather and the cool tone of white and light colors, I did not think much about the many choices here. Neither did I think I needed them. I went to school as a student. It should be a simple life. At the same time I recognized it was very nice to have choices.

Looking at the huge space around me and stores filled with a mountain of things, I had to admit to myself that gradually this picture of reality turned out to match well with the image of America I envisioned. *Everything was over the top.* At this realization, all these *things* and all this new space made the experience all the more American to me. The thought that "Yes, I *am* in America" started to become more and more a constant part of my physical and emotional bearings.

5. PERCENTAGE

FTER TWO WEEKS IN AURORA, I flew to Salt Lake City. I met another uncle, Sim, and his wife, Hồng. Uncle Sim has siblings living all over the globe: one or two in France, one in Denmark, two in California, and three others in the same city with him. Many of them went abroad to study in the sixties.

When the Vietnam War ended in 1975, getting into and out of Vietnam became impossible. The ones studying and living abroad remained where they were.

Twenty years after that, tinkering enough in both their front and back yards, the U.S. and Vietnam shook hands again. The siblings living in the U.S. sponsored their parents and a few remaining siblings in Vietnam to come to America for family reunions. Uncle Sim came to the U.S. for this reason. His family and his brother's settled in Salt Lake City where their two other siblings were already established.

Uncle Sim is a close relative both in blood and in spirit. His grandfather and my dad's grandfather are brothers. When it comes down to their generation, my father and my uncle Đình, uncle Sim and several of his siblings are around the same age. They went to school around the same time and shared some French-speaking background. In their adulthood, French cultural influence in Vietnam was completely overshadowed by the unpredictable war between the U.S. and Vietnam, and then replaced in most part by

American movies and literature. Familiarizing themselves with Elizabeth Taylor, James Dean, Audrey Hepburn and Gregory Peck, Hemingway, Arthur Miller, James Joyce, Tennessee Williams and Kerouac, Steinbeck and Faulkner, uncle Sim and his generation adopted a new language and culture.

To many youngsters like us they symbolized the good old days that diffuse some exoticism of French and American cultures. I used to envy them for knowing both foreign languages and cultures. Every time they hung around, we would hear pompous laughter and some French and English words. The sound of French words rolled like honey on their tongue we wanted to lick the sweetness right off. Then one of them would drop an American name, and the rest jump on it. They talked about Audrey Hepburn or Kerouac like critics. It sounded smart, civilized, and prestigious. *I want to talk about Audrey Hepburn or Kerouac like critics as well*, I dreamed. And their laugher and jubilant chatting, *those*—like they echoed from a mysterious seductive world of harmless joy we all indulged in once in a while. All to remind ourselves that such things as prestige and civilization were real even in this current brutal postwar existence of ours. A moment of forgetfulness, sometimes at our own or others' expense. Here, besides the fact that exoticism blinds us all, it is the French appeal in me talking, double-dosed with Americanism.

When I arrived in Salt Lake City uncle Sim and aunt Hồng proposed that I stay in the big house in which they lived all by themselves. Their twin sons were away at college.

Aunt Hồng had recently retired but uncle Sim was still working as a graphic designer at the *Salt Lake Tribune*. During the weekdays, with just aunt Hồng and me at home, the house was so quiet. I tiptoed here for fear of causing unnecessary noise, or messing things around, as the house was meticulously organized and clean thanks to aunt Hồng.

It was so quiet the air seemed to crack when I moved. I heard it breathe.

I could not help putting the image of noisy and crowded Sài Gòn next to one of Salt Lake City. In Sài Gòn, when darkness covered and everybody in the neighborhood was asleep, the night awoke. One could hear the wind blowing and the leaves whistling. Well, during my time, before the air conditioning era, we had French wooden doors and windows, the type that had small panes that reached the floor. You opened them in the middle, swung both your arms at full strength outward, and voila. When closed, all the space in between the panes ensure maximum air circulation for the house.

In the middle of the night, one could be startled by the sound of the cats running on the roof calling for mates. I was particularly scared by this. Either fighting with one another for the sake of fighting or for a mate, their meowing shrieked and pierced the dark night. It sounded like a ghost baby hysterically crying: "Mommy! Mommy!"

If lucky, one would be put to sleep to the sound of the soft rain dancing on the silver wavy steel or clear blue polycarbonate roof and brushing on the tiled floor of the balcony. Lying on the wooden floor behind the wooden French doors that separated myself five feet away from the balcony, I could hear the rain very clearly. It was a symphony of Vietnamese rain.

When not that blissful, it was the pouring and smashing rain that throbbed the night. Sometimes during the rainy season, roaring wind screeched through the blades of the wooden doors and windows. And thunder tore off the open space and flashed through the room. The storm arrived. Either with steel or polycarbonate roof, a storm equaled an army of percussionists playing military music who are summoned to torture your ears through the night.

Fortunately, kids were quick to wake and to sleep. Or one got used to it.

A lot of time the rain smelled fresh. Sometimes stinking heat evaporation and trash in the sewer mixed in the puddled water on the street. The stench filled the air.

Quiet would be the inviting rap of a vendor offering midnight snack on a dry hot day. One could hear him riding a bicycle. Without using his voice, he simply beat the two bamboo sticks together. *Tap-tap-tap. Tap-tap-tap.* Then they faded. If one needed his services, one had to hurry to the door and call out to him, or he was gone.

With the vocalist type, two to four words only, he was loud enough and yet not disrupting. *Noodle soup, anybody! Hủ tiếu đây!* The phrasing was a little bit of a staccato, but more subtle. Like an exclamation mark in the air.

That was the sound of the night in Sài Gòn. Imagine what the day was like! That is why many people believe Sài Gòn never sleeps. Here, it was the American kind of quietness, in the house, during the day, that I would get used to. Almost too peaceful to be real.

I liked uncle Sim and aunt Hồng's house a lot. Full of books and artwork. On all the walls, he displayed his own paintings and those of his friends, his digital artwork, and pictures, prints, multi-media works. They were strategically and artistically arranged. Airy, pleasant, and very rich in atmosphere. The house had many textures and was profuse with inspirations. *A world of one's own taste and design.* It reminded me of the promising journey I was taking, that if I worked hard I would eventually have it all—a basic American dream. I felt even more anxious about going to BYU to start my own adventure creating my own new world, if not immediately then the sooner the better.

After a few days of idleness, I pressured uncle Sim on the issue of driving me to Provo. "Why do you want to go there so early?" he asked. "To get ready for school," I told him. He made no immediate comment on that and paused for a second. His eyes tweaked a little, hardly enough to show any emotion. The smile on his face seemed to pause, out of surprise maybe, or pity, I was not sure. It was long enough for me to realize that it was I who was ridiculous to want to prepare for school more than a month ahead. I would be going to graduate school. What was there to prepare? What would I do at school, anyway? Only later did it strike me that I should have celebrated life in America with him and aunt Hồng instead of being single-minded about school. If I was not uber-nerdy, I was over-the-board naïve.

Well, I have a story about that.

Two years before I left for the U.S., I came across a book the title of which I still remember, *The American Way*, but not its author. It was a community college textbook that explained some basic characteristics of American people such as honesty and pragmatism—in a rather simplistic way, now that I think about it. The author talked about the early settlers who explored newfound lands and built their own houses out in the wilderness. It was all about self-reliance, independence and freedom. They forged their character out of ruggedness. They built an American system based on trust. *I like independent people. I consider trust essential in human relationships. And who does not love freedom?*

I found these ideas very impressive. (By the way, independence, trust and freedom were not issues we talked about openly in communist Vietnam back then, except along the line of indoctrination.) With little I knew about America, I treasured the book as a guide. The adventure into American land sounded so romantic and empowering I was ever since so anxious to start my own exploration. I had no idea what an American university was like. I just knew that the moment I got to America I needed to go to the library to read a lot of books, to be prepared for my adventures. I had an obsession with the written word that I will talk about later.

Facing my naivety and not wanting to beat my over-enthusiastic learning desire to a pulp, uncle Sim said: "I already contacted my friends over there about hosting you for a day or two while you look for a room. They should let me know in a few days."

A couple of days later, uncle Sim and aunt Hồng drove me to Provo. The city is forty-five minutes south of Salt Lake. "Are we going to your friends' house?" I was curious. The thought of staying with strangers, for the first time in my life, disrupted my heartbeat. "No. My friends live near Provo and they know this couple in Provo, Mr. and Mrs. Bá, who will help you." *So I am not even staying with his friends but with friends of his friends'. How strange.*

And generous, too! There is no way Vietnamese like us, living in an extended family, were able to squeeze a stranger into our space. No one moved around in my time to become a stranger, anyway. *Americans are truly friendly and generous, as I heard.* I envied the abundance that made them so.

At first sight, Mr. and Mrs. Bá looked different. They are bigger and taller than your average Vietnamese. Their dark skin and rugged built reminded me of those honest people who work hard to make it in life. They dressed casually. The muscles on their body must be very relaxed because their faces looked as if they were pampered and ready to smile.

Mr. and Mrs. Bá came to this snow land in the mid eighties as boat people refugees, already in their thirties, completely empty handed. After twenty years working multiple jobs, they not only paid off their house but also possessed several rental properties. They had a son, who was married, with a child, and his family lived ten minutes away from them. Mr. and Mrs. Bá recently bought another house which they gave to their daughter, Chi. Chi was a bit younger than me and single at the time. "She would be able to help you with whatever you need as far as school is concerned, and more," they said. "Her house is only a couple of minutes away from here on foot." Their southern accent sounded sweet and reassuring, making even a stranger like me feel safe and comfortable.

So that was where I would spend the night.

Vietnamese people often talk about how friendly and generous our Southern kinsmen are. Everything about Mr. and Mrs. Bá, who were from Gò Công, be it their behavior or speaking manner, bespoke the reputation of which I was on a receiving end. These common traits they share with the Americans didn't catch my attention even when I had acknowledged their good nature. Dwelling on comparison and contrast to extract differences to reach understanding was the lifeline I seemed to have created long before my arrival to America. For many years here, I stuck to it, embracing the pros and ignoring the cons in this way of thinking.

Chi was back from work late. I stayed at Mr. and Mrs. Bá's house past dinner time before she came and picked me up. Together we walked to her place via the back road across the dirt path in her parents' garden.

It was so dark I could hardly see my way, and so quiet. Cautiously and slowly, I walked.

A house in the city with a garden is a dream for people from Sài Gòn like me. They drool over just the sound of it. Besides, what is freer and more self-sufficient than to grow and to pick your own vegetable and fruits—*The American Way*. The salivation is true when I lived in Vietnam, it is more so nowadays when alarming news about poisonous food items from China flooding Vietnamese markets scared us away from the TV screen. Food safety is one terrifying daily concern, among much more serious ones, for the Vietnamese in the country. It is one 'tiny' cost to pay for living next door to a bully and imperialistic neighbor. But back to the fruit picking in the garden. The funny thing is that most Americans do not generally pick their own fruits in the back yard. They are so familiar with the sizes, tastes and textures of store-bought fruits that those in the yard fail to meet their expectation. Food is abundant and affordable, it is easier to buy it.

As I was crossing Mr. and Mrs. Bá's garden, keeping in mind the ideas about the American way, I was pretty hyped up on the self-sufficiency and freedom concepts. Around me, dark shapes of plants and herbs and trees made me so curious. In my head, a roller-coaster carrying a single thought raced: *People around the world love America for a good reason. It is a land of dreamers and fulfilled dreams.*

In the meantime, Chi charged ahead and I tried to stay close by. The first things I noticed about Chi were her penetrating eyes. Piercing straight at me, they were bright and kind. And her hair was blacker than the night over here. I know Americans look at us and say Asian people all have black hair. Well, I am Vietnamese;

black is a correct concept but there are different shades of black in the color of our hair. Mine would be black in American eyes. Putting it next to Chi's, it is brown in Vietnamese eyes.

I heard the insects calling. There was no sound of people talking. I don't remember whether Chi said anything. I heard only dry air mirroring quietness. Past Mr. and Mrs. Bá's garden, we reached the public lane. Nobody was around at this time of the night. *Just like the countryside in Vietnam, how interesting.* Normally, I would not have taken this road, simply because in Sài Gòn, I was used to the well-lit crowded streets full of people and noise. A dark quiet one could mean potential trouble somewhere along the way. But it was definitely different here. As a big-city girl, once again I was reminded that nature was a comforting part in everyday life in America.

The short-cut saved us a minute or two. Before long we reached Chi's house and entered through the patio door. "I just moved in about a month ago and still have a lot of unpacking and decoration to do," Chi spoke Vietnamese with a light American accent, mixing in some English here and there. We hung out in the kitchen a little, then went to bed.

The following morning, I woke up and went to the living room. Now that it was bright, the house revealed its nice features. The living room was large with a high ceiling, and big windows lined around. "Good morning." My self-tour was interrupted as Chi walked out of the bedroom and greeted me. "Let me show you around."

In one corner of the room by one huge window, there was a cozy sitting area where Chi had a Buddhist altar, a meditation pillow and a temple block on the floor. "I practice Buddhism and try to pray everyday when I can," Chi said. On the opposite side of this section, there was another intimate nook with a cushioned couch and a table. Chi had arranged small pots of plants and flowers along the window ledge. "This is the reading area," Chi said. "It could be a nice spot to sit and have tea, looking out to the yard as well."

"It is perfect," I told her. We were speaking in English. I noticed that many Vietnamese Americans switch back and forth. I thought nothing about the mixing at the time, but a micro instance of criticism surged. Suddenly bilingualism was annoying. When two languages at two strikingly different ends of a spectrum occupy the same zone, their underlying contrasting cultures and mannerisms have to be pushed to the surface for the final products. The mental factory has one hell of a chain of productions to shuffle and to process. It is not a very nice mesh. Instinctively, I prefer that people stick to one language.

Somewhere in the back of my mind, this should have reminded me of the way Vietnamese people have continued to reinvent themselves throughout history every time they are in contact with a foreign force; of my grandfather's generation speaking and mixing French and Vietnamese; of my father's generation concocting French, English and Vietnamese; all of which I used to adore. Or the post-1975 socialists and communists who blended Vietnamese and Russian. Only that this time it was happening to me—I was able to mix English and Vietnamese. I should have been elated instead. Not knowing why I felt the discomfort and whether this feeling would go away or not, I simply made a mental remark of the situation.

Upstairs in the spacious attic there was another room and a full bathroom. The tour ended at the greenhouse behind the kitchen where Chi still had tons of unopened boxes waiting to be sorted out, and the back yard beyond. It was a nice house with much potential. It zipped me back to my dream about a place of my own and reminded me of my pressing situation.

I told Chi I needed to look for a place to stay. Truth was that both she and her parents offered me a room in their house with low rent and good company. "I would cook for you. Cooking a family meal for two or three is all the same to me," Mrs. Bá explained. I found this part of the offer the most tempting.

"Thank you so much. It is so nice of you," I told them. "It would be so fun staying with you. But honestly, I have not been on my own before and really look forward to that experience. I hope you understand. I would love to visit you once in a while, though." I told them so apologetically. What I did not disclose was that, deep down, I considered my lone journey in the U.S. a chance to fulfill my craving for independence and freedom in the American way. I had waited for this moment my whole life and would not let anything or anyone spoil it.

"Stop by anytime," Mr. and Mrs. Bá told me. "We always have Vietnamese food here."

They were the only Vietnamese family in Provo at the time.

With Chi's help, I found a furnished room in a house with a "grandma" as advertised. It turned out to be a quiet, cute, cozy, little house with a cozy, cute, little garden. The room was decent and neat, and the house very clean. The owner did not at all look like a 'grandma' as I had imagined. She looked very young. I felt comfortable with her in this house. I told 'grandma' Joyce right away that I would take the room. I wrote her a check for the security deposit, and moved in the next day. A few houses down the road was the bus stop, which was very convenient as that would take me to school everyday. Across the street from the bus stop was a grocery store. It could not be better than this.

After Chi dropped me off at my new place with the luggage, I started unpacking and arranging my room. The two heavy suitcases became much more loaded when I weighted in my burning desire to 'settle down' in a place of my own. For the first time ever, this room was my own world where people needed to knock and ask for permission to enter. I could even make up a whole set of entrance rules. *My own room! I have my own room!* I wanted to jump up and down. For my generation, many growing up in an extended family, this private world was a dream.

I put books on the shelves. Hung clothes on the hangers on the left side wall of the closet. The space right below was for shoes. I ran out of hangers. I folded jeans and extra clothing, including a few *áo dài* and a Western dress, and piled them on the shelf above the hangers. Then came all the accessories and souvenirs, which I laid out neatly in the chest of drawers. I emptied every little thing into the drawers and there was still a lot of space in the last one. I went through the two suitcases in no time. They were now empty while my excitement about the new place remained full. I had no picture or painting or anything to hang on the wall. There was basically nothing else I could do. I felt incomplete. So far I got exactly what I wanted, had come to America for school, had a room of my own. And yet, this little world now seemed too small. Or too huge: I had put almost my whole world in Vietnam into two suitcases and taken it here. It fell through space like a particle of dust. Something was missing. *I should have brought more things. With more things I could easily use a bigger room.* One strand of thought seemed to mold itself out of my head. Was it greed that already started to grow in me. *Now that I have a little taste of the American dream, I want more? And what is that ambiguous sense of smallness or largeness?* I took note of my feeling, a little disappointed at my own disappointment. Right now a bigger room was not going to happen as I was ready to adopt a simple student life in the new land. I tucked this mental note away.

Overall, I felt very comfortable and energized in the new room as it was.

I came out to talk to my new housemate. Joyce showed me how things worked around the house; how to handle recycling; the section of the fridge reserved for me; and how we split utilities costs. She looked very young for someone in her mid fifties. A widow for many years, she enjoys her five children and a lot of grandchildren, many of them living nearby. Her short hair was above the shoulder, the tight curls pressed upon her nape. She has very fair complexion and the silver hair made her face look even brighter. Joyce smiled a lot and I thought she was very gentle and kind.

Everything seemed to work out well for me so far and I felt blessed.

I would spend more than a year and a half of my life here with Joyce, my Mormon grandma housemate.

* * *

The following day was Sunday. Joyce went to church. I went grocery shopping with Chi at Walmart. It took me more than two hours to acquire everything on the list. As the cart filled up to the rim, a grandiose sense of satisfaction and some anxiety uncannily took over me.

In the store, scanning all the *things* in oodles lining and stacking the shelves I found products I knew how to use; then there were gadgets I had no idea what they were for; and there came items I could not imagine actually existed. My mind was like a rubber band stretching to accommodate the new things. It was incredible, I admitted to myself, to be submerged in the world of materials where one's imagination was actually tested against the horizontal line of reality and sometimes bounced perpendicularly against the vertical wall of inspiration to get out to space. I could easily see how and why people enjoyed and were addicted to a materialistic life. Vietnamese overseas who visit Vietnam talk constantly about it, that you could find anything in America. Now I understood. I thought back on the moment of greed I had when in my new room and realized that goods have corrupting properties. See it, touch it, feel it. You'll be addicted to it. The accumulation of newer and newer products day after day filled up your space and time giving you a sensation of fulfillment that clogged your day and night. The choices are limitless out there for people to explore. For many, that was a sure sign of a healthy democracy. I thought so, too, at the time—that a good government at least made the citizens happy with a satisfying material life.

Yet I could not help wondering whether people were aware of the limitation of free choices. When in Vietnam, I would argue to death the preposterousness of putting 'limitation' and 'free choices' next to each other. Living in a culture where 'no choice' was standard in different aspects of life, I imagined the ultimate phase to freedom and democracy would be the presence and maintenance of unlimited choices for the people. That too many choices could be a solution that in turn opened up to another problem was beyond my thinking. Now, after acquiring a cart-full of items, it occurred to me that choices came with knowledge, a certain familiarity with some basic social concepts, and responsibility. Choices in buying expanded to those political, professional or emotional decisions one made. Here in the U.S., everything is a matter of choice. *How do people know they made a right choice, and how is democracy in a country ensured and affected by the choices people made?* The latter question in itself was a big equation that disseminated various solutions. *You must know what you are doing to survive here then* was the thought I took with me as I pushed my cart out of Walmart.

Back at my place, it took Chi and me many trips from the car to the house to carry everything. I was not so much tired about the shopping as I was overwhelmed and over-excited by the influx of information being processed in my mind. For one, I felt comforted. A sense of vindication rose in me. I read the label: Serving size 4, Calories 180, Saturated fat 9%, Cholesterol 15%, Sugar 9g, Total carbohydrate 12g, Protein 6g. "Don't buy things that have ingredients you cannot pronounce," Vegetarian Chi alerted me to the food labels. "Don't buy food with high sugar or sodium content." Considering it was 2001, that was so smart of her. California became the first state to ban soft drink sales in grade school in 2003. And high-calorie soft drinks were removed from all U.S. schools in 2006. I remember watching educational messages on TV begging people to read food labels for health information around this time.

Me in 2001, eliminating unhealthy substances, I embraced the food world. In my head, the ingredients, numbers and percentages jumbled themselves out into weave-able lines I could use to create my own gastronomic textures. I did not have to rely solely on my common sense, my folkloric knowledge of food and eating habits to pick items anymore. *Somebody here definitely knew very well how to spread information, and nobody needs to catch the wind for that.* I thought about the *trúng gió*—literally translated as 'catch the wind'—mentality in Vietnam.

"Mr. Hai who lived at the end of the lane died yesterday," I heard somebody said. "What is the cause?" I asked. "He *trúng gió!/* caught the wind!" At one time in my formative years, most news of death sounded exactly like that. A sudden death was always because of *trúng gió* because people couldn't explain how he was alive yesterday and dead today in his sleep. We were deprived of public health information, and all kinds of information, back then. Nobody talked about the difference between a heart attack and a stroke. A sudden death in either way was same same. *Trúng gió* solved all the problems.

Still studying the label I thought to myself: *All the power to science! I like how logic and science are a foundation of life here in the U.S.*

Suddenly, I realized I needed needles and thread next time I went out for a shopping spree with Chi. *Ridiculous!* A silent laughter leaning towards mockery fired off before I could jam it with my reasoning. It had not occurred to me that these would be items on my shopping lists in America, in glorious America! Not willing to add any crude elements into my American Dream, I swallowed this needles and thread reality hard.

The shopping experience ultimately could be weary. I heard that American people moved around a lot. For one who mobilized for the first time, I wondered how they did it.

In front of me was a table full of food items. I started to sort out things around the kitchen and prepared for the cooking. I peeled onions and carrots, diced them, sliced celery and mushrooms, cut the pork and cabbage. I prepped everything into separate containers. At one point, Joyce was back from church. I heard her get in her room. A few minutes later, she came out to the kitchen and gasped: "Wow, it is a lot of things you are cooking there."

"I cook for the whole week," I told her. Amidst this battlefield of food stuffs and my weekly gastronomical duties, I felt an undeniable delectation of having a kitchen all to myself. *So this is what American independence must feel like.* I tried to enjoy every single second of the experience believing that whatever I was doing, it was a new world I was forging for myself. Every little detail counted and it all tied back to me, affecting the kind of experience I was going to have.

Finally, the cooking was done. Exhausted, I sat down at the table and chewed on the feeling. Something was unsettling. Whatever I was doing here was temporary. After putting in a lot of work to settle down I would move again. I would be back to Vietnam sometime soon. Something rootless was lingering. I have heard stories about old Vietnamese who refuse to move away from the house they have been living in since birth. "This is the land where my ancestors were buried and I will be one day, you know," the narrative goes. "Leaving all that behind to move to a new place is cutting me from my root." I used to consider those people stubborn and old-fashioned. They possess the kind of spirit that ties us down to stagnancy and backwardness. *Is the sense of rootlessness I am feeling now a part of what those old people feel, then?*

I thought about American people. When in Vietnam reading about their mobility, I envied the fact that they could just pick up and move while in Vietnam in my time it was such an enormous deal, sometimes even an impossible thing. I heralded the American capability to move forward in life as a sign of progress. Forsaking the old place to move to a new place for a job, American people would build a home, and grow a root anew each time. I was only concerned about the logistical aspect of the action. Experiencing now the unstable and ephemeral sense in me, I understood it required more than the physical endeavor. I needed some mental switch as well to ease into a new life. How did they do it? I would want to know what that feels like.

Around 2008 I heard about white American friends taking a new job where they could be near their family so that their children could spend time with the grand-parents and the cousins. I was shocked at the news. I had not recognized that happy family relations had become a much encouraged element for social stability and productivity in America. I did remember that, at the turn of the century, high tech corporations such as IBM or Google started talking about creating a friendly and relaxing environment for their employees. They allowed them to work at home, provided childcare in the workplace, extended parental leaves, designed bright and stimulating workspace, and so on. All to create a healthy family life and to boost productivity. This kind of thinking has become an established practice nowadays in many workplaces. At about this same time, Vietnamese parents began sending their kids abroad, to Singapore, Australia, Canada, or America for college education. And they did so in measurable numbers. They evolve, too. It is a trend in Vietnam these days for wealthy parents to send their children to Australia, Canada or the U.S. at a younger age, for high school education. Since 2015 Vietnam has become the top market, percentage wise, of foreign students coming to the U.S. The parents have to spend a fortune on that, on top of their constant worry about losing the children to American temptations. So at the time when American corporations join families together, Vietnamese people break them apart. Each has very legitimate reasons to do what they think fit for their own situation. It is still ironic, though, how history spins its own course and teases us all. And I am left with my own to contemplate.

In 2001 I still thought the ability to cut ties with one's roots was essential for moving forward in life. I sat in the kitchen seeing the bright summer light fade into the late evening. The smell of food was lingering. Ten o'clock, everything dimmed. I turned more light on and cleaned up, ready to call it a day. Already I started to forget what I felt earlier about the rootlessness and family. As a new student in the U.S., I did not at all think in terms of what I brought with me and what I left behind. When I last saw my friends, some said: "Don't come back. Get married and stay over there." *Who does not want to live in paradise* was their reasoning. I knew for sure I would remain in the U.S. until I got my PhD. Everything and everybody would be there when I came back. If not, that's life. I would move on. My parents in Vietnam wanted *paradise* for me. I wanted this trip for myself. Less than a month in the U.S., I did not miss anything, yet. Besides, my younger brother was in the U.S. finishing his PhD degree—I was not alone. My first priority was to study. This goal anchored me in American steel and kept me away from all distractions, good and bad alike.

6. LAMENTER

KNOWING THAT MY SENSE OF direction is off, I was very nervous thinking about getting on the bus the first time, especially when I did not have a bus route map. Forget about the internet. It was 2001, unless you were well-off, your best bet for home use was dial-up with NetZero. This kind of service allowed you free internet access up to a hundred minutes a month. When your time was up, you paid a huge amount of money or waited till next month for more internet use. Good luck counting your minutes. They flew.

I did not have my own phone yet so even NetZero was out of the question. Joyce confirmed with me that the bus right outside was on route to BYU campus. "It is a short ride around ten minutes. And don't worry. It is very simple. You could not miss it."

I took her word for it but could not suppress the worries.

I tried to look on a bright side. When in Vietnam I heard that the bus was not popular because everybody here had a car. My exposure to public transportation could be an interesting experience. I became excited and prayed for it to be trouble-free.

Next morning, I got on the bus. The thought of getting lost terrified me.

Back home, Sài Gòn is a compact crowded city. Even when I got lost in some alley, I felt reassured to be enveloped in a cozy space that matched my size. The alley would eventually lead to a big road

I recognized. In the university campus where I taught, there is one way in and out. The chance to get lost in Sài Gòn was minimal and I kept control at all times.

Now the huge space and no pedestrians on the street meant that getting lost equaled to my losing control for the first time in my life.

About eight or ten minutes later with my heart still jumping in my chest, the driver called out to let me know BYU campus was here. I thanked the driver and got off the bus. As soon as my feet touched the ground, I looked up and right in front of me were structures I did not know what to make sense of. I was not sure how to proceed. There was no main gate, meaning a long fence and a big two-door iron gate as an entrance to a university the way it is in Vietnam. Instead, I saw buildings, small pathways, open space and lots of trees. I felt like being in a maze. *The campus is surely vast. Should I take left, right, or straight?* I found the experience very confusing.

I had to do something, anyway. I went straight hoping to run into someone to ask for directions to the Kennedy Center. Soon enough I saw a student. He advised me to turn left at the grey tall building, left at the fountain, then straight, and et cetera. I did not take notes as it would be easier and faster to ask again. So I thanked the guy and walked on.

At the point where I was supposed to go straight as told, the paths in front of me were not really 'straight.' They were more like curving left and curving right. How interesting! I began to think the guy did not know what he was talking about. Or I had lost my way. *No, probably not everybody knows what they are talking about*, I concluded, somewhat surprised that *I* questioned a white guy. Before that moment, I never thought that American people were wrong. (Yes, I was that much brainwashed!) In all the movies I watched in Vietnam, from all the stories told by Vietnamese Americans I know at home, and from tattletales floating everywhere, Americans are kind and friendly, they are heroes and inventors and problem solvers. How could they be wrong! Though quite certain the white guy gave me the wrong directions, I quickly dismissed this red flag in my mind.

Facing the curving paths, I stopped somebody else for help, and got directions to reach my destination. I entered the building via the first door I found.

At the Graduate Office I completed the required paperwork for the new year, then looked for the same door to go back out. I found many. They all looked the same. I did not expect so many exits and entrances to each building. It was ridiculous that I came from a big city, in terms of population, with small space to get lost in a small city with huge space. Unable to tell which door I had entered I chose one and exited. Outside was not the path that took me here. It's like being in a labyrinth again. I began to think there was definitely some confusion in the hugeness of space in America. *It presents challenges. It tricks and taunts the mind.* I felt panicked. To be scared of being lost on campus was not my concern, because the friendly Americans would help me out. I was losing control. I stood there for a few seconds, thinking and sweating.

Then an odd feeling crept in. *What would an American do? How would they handle a new environment and a situation like this one?* I talked to myself. From American movies I watched at home, I had the impression that Americans were very good at handling themselves in all circumstances. *But that is not so important. How would one make a choice in a situation like this? They would probably do what I was about to do making whatever choice I was going to make, anyway. Remember, I wanted to come to America to learn about this country. Here I am. Just do it.* These thoughts flashed in my head.

I looked at the blue sky above my head, at the multi-story buildings in front of me, at the beautiful trees surrounding me, at the clean walkways under my feet. It was early afternoon. With a lot of time on hand before it got dark, it should be alright if I got a little lost. Determined to give myself a chance to 'explore' America, I decided to deal with my own fear. I was 29, too old, and too pathetic, to play peekaboo with America, but I was ready. *I would get used to it.* I walked straight ahead not knowing where I was heading. Walked until I saw the name of some building outside, then looked it up on the map I picked up at the office, and tried to find my way to the bus station. Along the way, I took my time to enjoy and admire the landscaping. An American university campus was my paradise where I could find a library with all the books I wanted to read and a world of knowledge that brought freedom to my starving soul. I had plans for the library another day. Today, I stopped to smell the flowers. Touched the leaves. Looked up and down the trees and the sky. Some people came to me and asked if I needed help, probably because they saw me looking around as if lost. I said no.

For what it's worth, I figured out one way Americans deal with huge space and what their mental experience might be like. Unawares, I counted a third dot connected.

Twenty-nine. It never occurred to me that 29 was pretty old to start a new journey in a new land. At that age, the language learning curve is coming to an end. Old habits settled. Behaviors cemented. Fortunately, I did not think about my age at all. If any, I was happy to get to America at 29 instead of 30 or 35.

I remember a conversation with two white American classmates after I turned 31. One was over forty and the other I did not know his age until he suddenly lamented: "Man, I am 25 and I feel so old and tired." I held my breath. For a second, reality seemed to hit me. *What is he going to say if he knows my ancient age! Am I old at 31? Do Americans think 31 is old? Probably they do.* The older guy tried to comfort him but he was not convinced; his gloomy look deepened. On my part, I quickly threw away the numbers, believing too strongly in the American spirit: It's never too late. I looked at the 25-year-old thinking how young he was, totally agreeing with the older guy that it must be the graduate school taking a toll on him. I felt in him the pain of betrayal living in a country that glorifies the splendor of physical youth. But I did not feel that in myself. How I felt depended on the comparative analysis I had in mind, a process of which I had no control by now. According to my analysis, being young in Vietnam, for most people, means being oppressed. The parents, grandparents, friends and relatives, teachers and neighbors, the in-laws and so on, all have their eyes on you. They are your around-the-clock counselors who keep telling you what you should and should not do, and intervene without notice, for better and/or worse. Caring so much about what they think and craving so much for their approval, at the same time hardly being encouraged to think for oneself and to take responsibility for one's action, young people are stuck in a cage of abusing care. The very lucky and strong ones can hope to counteract this attitude and start living their lives at 25. I'm talking about the super strong ones. The intervention could last your whole lifetime if you let it. Therefore, compared to their Vietnamese counterparts, young Americans are having a free ride and I'd prefer their way: to have my freedom, start making my own mistakes, to live and learn my life at 18. It's such a waste if they don't enjoy it. Even at 31 life only just started for me. So I pit the American and Vietnamese systems against each other to spin out my own value fabric, its crude quality being fit only for myself as I tried to edge my way in the new place. On second thought, maybe I should have told the lamenter this.

I did not get to the bus station until late afternoon. The first bus trip was a success. Very pleased, I allowed myself the pleasure of sightseeing on the bus.

Looking out the window Provo was a beautiful city. Tall magnificent trees lined both sides of the streets. Bright and colorful roses wove along fences. In the park, children were playing and laughing happily with their parents. It was a very peaceful picture of one afternoon in Provo. I checked my watch, ten minutes passed. Outside, the houses looked the same as the ones near my place. My stop should come up very soon, I reassured myself, not wanting to think that I was lost.

Twelve or fourteen minutes passed. The houses still looked the same. I thought I knew better. Now I was lost for real. Checking the map, I must have been in Orem. *Orem? What? Orem??? How on earth did this happen? The campus is gigantic and ten-minute bus drive, I go from Provo to Orem? How could I leave one city to enter another without even knowing it??? There is no way on earth I could get on a bus in Sài Gòn and ten minutes later I am in Biên Hòa! Things will look very different and I will know immediately. Besides, Sài Gòn is huge!* Perceptions and realities of old and new jumbled up. My heart rate was rising. It was getting dark. I reined in my fear and got off the bus. Again, it was 2001, cellphones were not a popular gadget, at least for someone in my situation. I walked to the nearest residential area and knocked on a random door.

A kid answered it. She could be five or six years old. She stood there and stared at me. "Hi," I said to her, "I am lost. Could you go tell your parents I need to borrow the phone?" She ran away and disappeared behind the door, leaving it open. Seconds later, a very young, beautiful, blond-haired woman appeared. "How can I help you?" she said. I told her I was lost and would like to borrow her phone to call for help. "OK," she said, then walked away and came back with a cordless phone.

I called Mr. Bá to request the big favor. I heard him and his wife giggle on the other end of the phone. He told me to wait and he would be there. I returned the phone to the kind woman, thanked her and waited on the street outside.

While waiting, I looked around the area. In this suburban housing district, there was no landmark to spike my memory. I thought it was bizarre that in a country iconized for individualism (in Vietnam, one of the first things youngsters like me adored about America was individualism), American houses follow the same code of subdued surface colors of gray and light blue. The whole block had the same type of two-story houses, identical in size and shape. In communist Vietnam, individuality is a no-no but people build their house in whatever style they prefer and paint it whatever color they choose. I did not learn at the time about the sense of conformity in American society and the assembly-line approach to housing construction. So thinking about the paradoxes in human life and straining my eyes for a landmark so I could revisit this place later as where I first got lost in America in a bus drive kept me entertained while waiting for Mr. Bá.

Ten minutes later, he arrived. I got in his car and we had a good laugh about my lost experience. Minutes after that I was back home. I swore to study the map and the landmarks. Throughout dinner I found myself thinking about why Americans wanted huge space.

7. WAS

A YEAR AT BYU WENT BY fast. In a few more months I finished my thesis.

When I first came, I was told what I had at BYU was "a true American experience," something I would not find elsewhere in the U.S. I believed that. I made good friends here the same way I did in Vietnam. There are dress codes at BYU that I also embraced because it was the same way I dressed in Vietnam. I took comfort in the fact that I fit in so well in America.

I knew nothing about Mormonism or where it stands in the religious scene in America. I simply observed and absorbed. What struck me the most about Mormon people was the public display of their belief. One professor started class with a prayer. I did not expect this but considered it an ultimate manifestation of freedom of expression in America.

My friends talked to me about their religion. I talked about life. Not a religious person in any way I embrace spirituality which I defined as a belief in some goodness out there. The Mormons' Heavenly Father was like a Supreme Power or a universal God to me. The philosophical rhythm folded in our conversations bonded us as our topics deepened and widened. We got to know each other beyond the socialization level, which confirmed my belief that, even though we could be so different, we could communicate effectively with one another to live in peace.

Everywhere, people were nice and kind. Then, after I had a chance to see other non-Mormon Americans around the country,

I noticed that the Mormons looked very bright. They just looked bright and happy to me. I attributed this to their spirituality.

All in all, I truly believed I was able to be myself at BYU, that I was appreciated and loved for who I was. The constant feeling of *I am home* accompanied me the whole time.

One day I received an email from my mom. At the end of the letter, she said: "You are like a fish in water. I am happy to see you like that."

It was true I felt like a fish in water in most ways, even when I was a lost fish in the ocean without a school of her own. Being a foreigner in the new land, time was a confusing element.

Everything in America had a deadline. Electricity, gas, water, telephone bills had deadlines. Papers and library books had due dates. So do credit card balances. Doctor appointments had time slots. We plan gatherings with friends on an agreed upon date, weeks or months in advance. There is something due everyday. Life is regulated by specific numbers. They branched wide. They angulated. They caged me in. To keep up with these numbers was stressful. And depressing in a way, as they made me feel confined and helpless in a box of time made out of lines. I stretched them out in my mind and all I saw was a long line punctuated with markers. I could only move from one point to the next on this flat line. How bizarre to walk on a flat line to go through life. I did not find a rhythm to it. Yet? This was American linear thinking, I figured. Back home, I was used to a sphere where I could jump everywhere. There were no due dates or deadlines. Around the end of the month utilities agents come to our house and collect the money without advanced notice of any kind. They knock on the door. If we are not around, they come back another time. Or we leave some money with our neighbor to pay the bill and get the receipt for us. If I was suddenly in a mood to see my friend, I walked or biked over. One time a bunch of us biked sixteen miles from Sài Gòn to Hóc Môn to see a friend who happened to be out. We pedaled back in the scorching heat pumping each push with stories that overflew our memory reservoir for forty years to come. Spontaneity was a scent of life. Nothing was pre-arranged as a mark on a calendar. Money, people, and time float fluidly. There was a sense of romance and relaxation in this way of living.

It took me a long time to figure out how to stay on the flat line and to appreciate its value, which was the lesson I learned in conjunction with my linguistic battle with time.

Monday morning, I met D. in our graduate office. "Did you have a nice weekend?" he asked. "Yes, I did." D. smiled, "Yeah, what did you do?" "I go ... went to visit a friend over by the park," I stuttered, feeling annoyed by the pause in my head. Ughh.

Ever since I arrived in the U.S., my battle with English verb tenses was ongoing. The moment I opened my mouth to talk or sat down to write papers, I found myself thinking hard to choose a verb, which sometimes has to be in the present and other times the past. I consumed seconds to clarify with myself: *That thing already happened—checked for past tense; This is still valid and going on—OK for present tense.* Conjugating the verb tenses before spitting them out became the routine spasm between me and English grammar.

In the Vietnamese language there is no requirement to conjugate verbs. There are a few denominations to indicate the present, the past and the future but which are not used all the time; the context plays a crucial role to clarify temporal indication. I would say that the Vietnamese language sounds present to me. There seems to be a seamless transition between temporal points that leads to the smooth mental transition back and forth in time.

In my mind, there was no demarcation that separated the past from what was happening in my life right now, as if Vietnamese people live-and-fight-and-die-and-pass-on-their-spirit-over-generations-seamlessly, that things evolve circularly, in whatever direction there may be, all sharing one point of return—life. Everything fuses into everything else, not leading forward as in a linear line, in periods of time the way I have seen history divided in American textbooks. I would recall an old story and did not have to use simple past. The use of the present tense made it seem more real. So, we conjure up events or stories of the past and talk about them as if they are facts of life and moral lessons to learn for all times.

In English, I need to be clear about the use of the tenses. I rely on my knowledge of English grammar to make it sound right, even when in my Vietnamese thinking it may not make sense. The confusion had nothing to do with English grammar and more with Western logical traits, the concepts of time and what they meant, as well as the adaptation of the mind that I myself needed to make.

As I moved along the more I thought about the time issue and the more back and forth I went between the two languages, the more confused I became linguistically, but more transcendent mentally.

An old friend died today; that person has already become: "He was a wonderful father." My instinctive reaction to the "was" would be: "How ridiculous! I just saw him yesterday." In my circular mind, a hundred years ago could still be present, today could not be the past. But yes, of course it could. Even a second ago *was* already the past.

It took me a long time to accept the logics of time in the English language, to get used to using the simple past this way. But I knew such a was would continue to shake me. Every time I read or heard an obituary, I couldn't help but hang on to the past tense verbs and freeze time, waiting. The verbs would ring in my ears like a drop of water that falls into a pond and ripples. I wait. Till they fall flat, sink in me, returning to the still surface, quiet, making me feel that the person was already, really, dead. Then everyday noise resumes.

There is nothing much I could argue about languages, except to accept them. I'm just glad that the linguistic journey opened my mind to a never-travelled-before world. Because of it, I came to realize that, by using the present tense in our language, Vietnamese people unwittingly use the past as an enormous resource to fuel the present. For many of us, glorifying the past in search of validity becomes our second nature. Vietnamese society could not evolve when people make it their destiny to revere the past—which means keeping the status quo and remaining backward. In everyday activity, the way we treat older people and think about old age facilitates this mentality. Many Vietnamese begin to feel 'old' at forty seemingly getting ready for the later part in life. At fifty, they consider themselves 'mature' and 'experienced.' At sixty, they live on distributing free solicitation. They babble about life in a visualization of coming death and the final days on earth, as if they could feel the judgment day pumping in their chest. Unable to catch up with new ideas, concepts, technologies or values of the present in order to move forward, at the same time already revered by many as "seniors" with past experience to share, they hang on to the belief that they represent the wisdom of the past, that they live long enough to carry the whole past with them to puncture the future, that they simply know best. From them, dooming thoughts and negative commentaries spill out like commands of a losing general. "Oh, be careful with what you are trying to do. It is very difficult!" "But this project is so tough. How are you going to carry it through alone?" "I am afraid that you cannot persuade the department. You know how the system here works! Keep yourself in line." "I am afraid that if I make students work hard, they will write bad reviews of me and the department will take the classes from me." Blah blah blah. The sign of the past is easy to spot. The sentence usually begins with "but" or "I am afraid that."

When all they have is the past, there is a big 'but' on their head and they are afraid of everything. The present is messy and the future unthinkable. Giving (bad) advice is the easiest thing to do on earth, as Socrates told us so, and that is exactly what they do. This same spirit runs in the veins of many younger people who follow their seniors' lead.

There is a trend among many Vietnamese these days: In order to express their disappointment about how the communist government runs things, they dig up the rotten corpse of the South Vietnamese government and put it on the pedestal; as if they want to resurrect it as a new government. This is a standard historical case of "Human memory is short." We all suffer this kind of amnesia once in a while when fact checking becomes overwhelming. Last time I checked, those dead presidents or generals the Vietnamese now glorify were the same ones Vietnamese people at wartime went on the street to protest against, for their brutal tactics against civilians, their incompetent leadership, or their pure corruption. For anyone who could see the faults of the South Vietnamese government back then as well as those of the current communist's, I want to tell them that the Vietnamese people's task in this twenty-first century is to build a better system than both the old and the current one combined to sustain itself in the next century, if it is to survive. Many of us perceive the past as an insurmountable puzzle that blocks our sight of the present, our vision for the future and the path there. It absorbs all our energy.

As I was etching my way in America I found that the inherited manifestation of Vietnamese mental maneuvers with time had dulled and truncated my capacity to think creatively to get where I wanted to go. I was circling in the space of the past so often I was locked in it. That is why over here, as I dovetailed America in a search for progression to spearhead the foggy past-present in which I had lived all my life, I came to appreciate the clear-cut tenses of the English language. Maybe the past should be so clearly marked as dead and left alone.

The learning curve made me realize the impact of language use on identity and personality. As someone who writes in both English and Vietnamese trying to bridge the gap between the past and present in language as well as in reality, I have oscillated between the two languages to find my way. I have come to feel both English and Vietnamese as an extended part of myself and an integral part of my identity. But right before this happened, to make the learning curve more interesting, soon after school started, American friends and people I came across began to ask me about the 'Vietnam War.' The first time that happened, I was a little disconcerted and told them: "How interesting that you call it the 'Vietnam War,' because in Vietnam we call it the American War. After all, Americans invaded my country and started the war." They were shocked to hear that.

So, the 'Vietnam War' was one of the first questions they asked me the moment they knew I came from Vietnam. Not just the Vietnam vets, my classmates who were younger also talked about the war with me. One, two, many times. In my battle for the right verb tense to respond to them, I noticed the contradiction between the American question about the Vietnam War and my observation that American people think about the present and the future most of the time. I did not know then that the Americans having issue with the Vietnam War only reflects deeper problems American society bears within itself.

I wracked my brain for a memory of the so-called Vietnam War that Americans talked so much about. I don't remember my friends and me talking about this war in Vietnam. We grew up after the war ended in 1975. We absorbed socialist teachings, to a certain degree depending on each one's family background, but we carry no war memory. I left Vietnam with a light heart, suffocated mind, but no war memory.

Living in an extended family in Vietnam, around the times of death anniversary gatherings, I would often hear adults tell ghost stories from wartime evacuations, or tales of relatives fighting in the jungles against the French and the Americans. I remembered being fascinated by the fact that, friends or foes during the war, they were now family and relatives, remembering mutual loved ones and sharing memorable stories of the old times. All these stories were like folktales, not my war memory to be nostalgic about, to think about, or to deal with.

So the American obsession with the war was perplexing. I got curious. I began checking out books about the so-called Vietnam War from the library.

Facts and stories about the war from both sides, especially the pain, for the first time seared my mind. Loud and silent screams of soldiers, bombarded bunkers, veteran nightmares and traumas, torture methods and victims, civilian sorrows and pain, napalm and cluster bombs, broiling trees and burning bodies, maimed children, and more became imprinted in me as if old slices of a country's war memory were implanted in my brain anew. After I closed a book, I would sit frozen like a body with brain death. Tears streak my face. James Hillman said that there is an insatiable thirst and a magnetic suction in the force of war that, once started, sets in motion the whole uncontrollable cycle in the human mind and human society. The Vietnam War books ignited such a force in me. The new readings turned me into a war embodiment with recurring nightmares, for days.

Of course I learned about American war crimes towards Vietnamese people previously at school. But when one has to study to memorize things for tests, it is no learning at all. I became almost oblivious to the pain of our own people, except in the case of Agent Orange. The graphic horror caused by this evil-inducing chemical is seen and felt by most Vietnamese regardless of their political inclination. So, back home reading Bảo Ninh's *The Sorrow of War* in Vietnamese I did not feel anything. There was nothing special about the American War. We sacrificed and eventually secured victory just like we did in previous wars. Within the big family, war history dons a familiar outfit: many of my relatives died during the war, many came back sick, others returned safe and sound. At death anniversaries we gathered around and talked about both memorable and horrible experiences of war, and we returned to our everyday life. It was the same circle Vietnamese people went through handling the Chinese, the French, the Japanese, and now the Americans. Surrounded constantly by live artifacts of war from both sides I perceived nothing different or special about Bảo Ninh's experience with war. Somehow the novel became a big deal when it was translated into English and received high praise abroad. That is the main reason it caught our attention and me picking up the Vietnamese book in the first place. Still, I read it and felt nothing. What I later learned about the different reactions from the two societies when it comes to the Vietnam War is this: *Basically, in Vietnam there is no guilt, there is no fuss.*

At BYU, I checked out Bảo Ninh's book and read it in English. By this time, I learned that one often feels differently about one's homeland once away from it. Distance provides perspective. Learning about the war from numerous points of view, and feeling viscerally the magnanimous pain of destruction by war compounded on Vietnamese soil, across geographical territory of Laos and Cambodia wrecking human lives leaving a trail of blood and sorrow across the continents, I appreciated his novel from a new angle. I came to believe in the significance of telling one's own story as part of a missing history that I did not learn back then at school. The excruciating images of the howling ghosts in the deep dark forest calling out for the lost souls of their comrades in Bảo Ninh's book have stayed with me ever since.

I also could not forget Tim O'Brien's *The Things They Carried* and the heavy footsteps of the soldiers wading through the rice paddies. After days of marching they came to a point where they literally had to tell themselves to move their feet forward one step at a time, left then right, without feeling, without meaning. Every time I take a walk in the park now I would hear those footsteps slopping on the muddy water.

At this point, like a passenger sitting in the back of the bus looking through the rear window, to borrow William Faulkner's image, who sees the passing landscape clearer and clearer the further away she goes, I saw, for the first time in my life—one growing up in a country that boasts thousands of years of history—a glimpse of what history was really like. And individuals like me are part of history as well.

I started to distinguish the past from the present and the future *and* the connections between them. In spite of the blurriness that still covered everything at the time, I began to build a bridge to crawl back and forth between the two countries, Vietnam and America, and between the past, the present and the future, thinking that I had found an invisible crystal path miraculously blown and fired in the air just for myself.

Standing on this bridge, I felt incredible to have had a chance to earn that kind of experience. With time, I acquired various perspectives into myself, my own language and culture, into American language and culture. More confident than ever about who I was and what I wanted to do, I naively thought at the time, I assumed the responsibility as a Vietnamese cultural ambassador to the world. Every experience I went through in America served as a training session to prepare me for that role.

8. SPACE

"**D**ID YOU KNOW THE RIDING board?" my good friend C. asked one day. We were in the same masters program at BYU and we clicked right the first time we talked. C. is a classic American girl whose blond hair slips into the secret dreams of many Asian boys. She is beautiful and with a gentle soul, caring so much about people around her and how to live a good life.

"No. What is it?" I responded.

"Oh, it is a board on which you find different pockets of paper sheets. Students leave notes about their trips to look for riders or drivers. Maybe you could find a drive to Denver," C. said excitedly. C. knew I was planning to visit my aunt in Aurora in the summer. I told her a cheap and fun way was driving as I would have an opportunity to see the country. Shared ride was a great idea.

I went to check out the riding board the next day and found a perfect riding solution. Two students would pick me up at my place, drop me off at my aunt's, like a door to door service, then ride off to their final destination in Denver. I was so excited about the coming trip. "Only in America!" I thought. Where else could we find friendly strangers who were willing to share and to trust one another enough to cozy up in a tiny car? Safety was not a concern in my American adventure at the time, the way it should be nowadays.

Sitting in the back seat through an eight-hour driving trip, I began another adventure. After all the talking was done, we needed some rest. At least that was how I felt. My mind needed some rest and some space after having to concentrate intensely on the conversation and constantly explaining things about my own culture and processing information shared by the new friends. Outside, the landscape of the American West rolled like a movie. The vast mountain ranges were pulling me up and dropping me on the immense plateaus. I searched my way into the deep forests being lulled by their murmurs. When I got out of the woods, I was meandering among the herds of cattle. Surrounding me was a rainbow of colors, so green, so dusty, so earthy brown and red. These scenes stretched for hours until they overflowed. My wandering mind began to fill with thoughts about the first settlers and their bumpy journeys to the new land here in the West, how they chose to build their home miles apart. Even in our time, we would go for so many miles before spotting a house.

I was submerged in the gigantic space that seemed to expand indefinitely. After a while, it stirred in me a feeling I had not experienced before.

Here I was in the car, as my mind needed space, I could not help thinking that the space my body occupied was there only as the much needed bubble to wrap around the mind—the bigger the better, just to keep the mind inside safe—as if to shield it from attacks and uncalled-for criticism that could hurt it, or worse, damage it for good. In my imagination, by the time the pilgrims settled in the new world, gone were the days when they were physically and mentally repressed and terrorized in the terrain of religious purge. In the new land, they found peace with themselves. Mentally, the scar was there. Who knows how long it takes to heal. A few hundred years is still too short a time to reassure the anxious heart and to temper the worrisome mind. Over time, the psychological pressure for safety molded into a national psyche of amassing space and materials as assurances of independence and freedom. And who can answer the question of how much space one needs to lay their mind at rest in the realm of peace and eternity. We cannot really measure how much space their mind needs, just as we cannot measure how far one can go with love or hate or bigotry. *That must be what the enormous space is for, a buffer of safety.* For a few seconds, those thoughts and feelings flooded me.

The experience was so sudden. Like a flash of light before my eyes that rolled the painter's hand to perform the last stroke to finish the *Lady of Liberty* painting. For those nanoseconds, I felt what it was like to be totally safe, to be totally free and independent, physically and mentally.

Flashes of images continued to shift through my head in torrents. As the car kept moving with the rhythmic sound of the engine and the rippling bumps of the tires sliding over the road fractures, I was rocking gently inside it totally absorbed in the confusing mixture of spaces and memories. The images of the tiny alleys in Sài Gòn kept surging together with the feeling of suffocation. The mornings and afternoons, driving on my motorbike alone around the city, to bookstores, to volunteer meetings, to day classes to study, to evening classes to teach, to gatherings, year after year, in utmost anguish and silence. I was looking for changes in thoughts, in behaviors, in the way of life but could not find them in anybody or anywhere. I was surrounded by noise and movements all the time in a very lively environment, yet they aimed at getting by and, for me, did not translate to 'actions' that led to somewhere or something new. I felt trapped in a thin bubble of space.

I had begun to travel alone. The anguish and silence shadowed me. The gnawing sense that something wanted to explode inside grew stronger.

I did not have language for all those experiences I went through back then. I only felt. There was no one with whom I could practice talking about those feelings to figure out the why's, the what's and the how's. They remained unarticulated feelings and thoughts, until now. Inside the tiny car, in the middle of nowhere in America in the far West, surrounded by utmost infinity of space, I was talking to *myself*, but *talking*, at the very least. I seemed to gain some understanding about the vastness of space in America. Everything suddenly made sense. The huge space around me stopped being a description in a textbook. The American sense of self-reliance and the desire for freedom were no longer concepts I could only think about—they made sense to me now. The price of independence, of uncompromised self-esteem—made sense. As I was crawling in a car driving through the limitless plateaus of the West and there was an infinite horizon outside the windows, for a split second, I experienced what it was like to be free as an American.

In Sài Gòn wrapped by crowdedness and trapped in a small space, my mind imbedded in small thoughts. There was no space to grow them. The horizon of freedom was beyond my reach. Every time we came across the scene of a thick mountain range or a pounding water fall in an American national park on TV, we exclaimed in delight: "How magnificent and magnanimous!" Face to face with the endless pine tree forests of Đà Lạt, we whispered: "How poetic, cozy and intimate!" We look at and feel American and Vietnamese nature differently, almost always glorifying the first and belittling the latter, even though we experience the first via television and the second in person. Why is that? I blamed the elongated skinny strip of land called Vietnam for the narrow-mindedness of the Vietnamese people. When and how did this perception about nature and space sip into my thinking and influence my perception? Is this way of thinking the reason why all my life in Vietnam I could not believe there was a living Vietnamese with a big heart and a great mind who knew what freedom was, let alone who could bring about freedom to my people?

I wanted to think that my criticism towards my own country and people was a momentary burst of anger for being denied freedom and free will for a long time. And more.

Concepts of space and freedom are not so rare in Vietnamese literature, always infused with a philosophical inclination. My favorite lines are from Nguyễn Công Trứ that my mom initially quoted and has since repeated in our family discussions: *Kiếp sau xin chớ làm người. / Làm cây thông đứng giữa trời mà reo.* "I would refuse to be a human in my next life, / I'd rather be a pine tree cheering in the sky." Nguyễn Công Trứ was a poet, a scholar, a mandarin, a general who devoted his life to his country. In 1858 Vietnam was on the brink of French invasion. At 80 he vowed to fight tooth and nail for the country's freedom and independence. He died at the end of the same year and has since been remembered as a hero and a person of high integrity. A pine tree represents honesty and integrity in a person. The reincarnation thought reflects Buddhist philosophy. Whenever looking for comfort, I cloaked my mind around the pine tree. The straight trunk in the sky portrays a way forward in the universe, in it time and space enclosed. Nature, in this image, was the last bastion of the human mind where it meets nothingness. To be a part of nature was to evaporate into nothingness. This way of thinking is traditional Vietnamese.

As I grew more restless, nothingness was the opposite of what I wanted and traditional thinking my enemy. At BYU as an American Studies student I repelled both. Instead of emptiness, I wanted to stir things up all the way to see for myself. And stirring things up paid off. The car adventure into the west enabled me to understand Thomas Jefferson's westward ambition and his saying: "Just give me land." The driving trip created a rare moment when I could step out of my own perspective and experience another's. It's precious. At the same time the enlightened moment belonged to the seductive world of harmless joy I could indulge in once in a while, this time at others' expenses.

It's true I found *The American Way* as I read in the book. The American West is still an attractive concept waiting for generations of newcomers to explore. It is also true that the officially touted American Way of living promoted to the world aims to justify the greatness of America, so that the truth about how the native Americans' lands were snatched, how the native people sold off to slavery, hurdled, killed, cornered and eventually dispersed to the reservations could easily be slipped under the carpet. Going West is still a great myth in the American dream fantasy that continues to mesmerize immigrants in their quest for paradise. It looms so large they become blind to the historical truth about the cruelly persecuted Indigenous peoples who once roamed the land.

The fact is many immigrants come and find gold here in America. Some find peace. Or freedom. Most others fall asleep in a landfill of temptations and lose themselves on their way to purchase the next SUV, the newly released handbag, or the latest smart phone. I did not come as an immigrant and did not look for a regular course to follow. Although I denied then that my perception of the American Dream was one directional, I was searching for a just way to go.

Since my arrival to the U.S. I was busy soaking in the newfound freedoms. For starters, they seem to be the right ingredients.

By the time I left BYU with a masters degree in American Studies, I had received a scholarship to pursue a doctoral degree in American History at Indiana University. I believed I could achieve whatever I set my mind on and was very confident in the way I was handling my life in the United States.

9. FATE

THERE WERE A HANDFUL OF Vietnamese and Vietnamese Americans in Bloomington when I first arrived, among them a math professor and his wife. "Do you know the Vietnamese American music professor here at IU?" the math professor asked me. "No, I don't," I said. "He is an interesting guy," he told me, then changed the topic. I had no idea what he was up to. His language is as coded as his personality of a mathematician who thinks and lives by numbers.

More than once, the math professor mentioned the Vietnamese American music professor. "I think you'd like him. Why don't you come talk to him to see what you think." Now I understood he was hinting at a match making for both of us. I told him I did not believe in match making.

Then a stranger thing happened. In my conversations with other Vietnamese in Bloomington, they also praised the music professor and encouraged me to get to know him. I became curious. I planned to attend a gathering organized by the Vietnamese Student Association, knowing *everybody* would be there.

On that day, I had class and could not make it there in time. When I arrived at the International Students House, not many people were around. They scattered in a few small groups. The discussion was over, the hanging out almost done and the food gone. People were saying goodbyes. I eyed the room and recognized the math professor, his wife and the music professor—I had checked out his profile on the website and knew what he looked like. I decided to join them in the last moments of their conversation. As I approached, the first thing I noticed about the music professor was the light pink shirt he was wearing, with a tie, underneath the jacket. I did not like a man in pink and felt turned-off right away. I slipped away before we had a chance to say hello, and forgot all about the event. Or so I thought.

Weeks later, I was still mulling over my reaction. I was very judgmental to have come to a quick conclusion about not wanting to get to know the music professor because he was wearing a pink shirt. Just by glancing at him and not having a moment to talk to him, I did not know what he was like. My reaction meant pure prejudice. It would only direct me to dark moments in life. I was very much aware of this. Then I thought about other times when I could have been prejudiced without even knowing it. Terrified to have stumbled upon an indecorous memory of my own, *But for this time, maybe I could do something to fix it*, a thought surged.

Equally motivating me was a conversation I had with an older professor and a wise mentor and friend at BYU who told me something I would never forget. He said that, by giving the other a chance to start a new relationship with me, I was giving myself a chance as well. The beauty of the expression, that I love, was the two-way logic in it that led to an action that facilitates responses and decisions from both sides; that by sitting alone massaging my own thoughts would not cut it, that only when our thoughts are exposed and tested could they lead to a sound decision.

This advice was the kind of optimistic practical American thinking that offers a fair and thorough solution to every party involved. It was very refreshing compared to the familiar hierarchical thinking I grew up with where men often think they are always right, and that women can hardly think right and are inferior. That's why the moment I heard the professor, the clear-cut American logic got to me instantly and stayed put. It turned out to be very good advice to cure the state of un-decidedness or any judgmental behavior that in my case I was unaware of until I zoomed into myself.

The American phrasing also made me think about the concept of fate.

Many Vietnamese friends I have talked to hold a belief that the best or worst thing that happened to them was pre-ordained. They either enjoyed their luck or endured the mishap. I often made jokes about that notion of fate with them, and they did, too. "Fate" is *số*, in short, or *số phận*, in full, in Vietnamese. As a homophone, *số* also means "number." So when people commented: "Oh well, that is fate!" I would ask: "What is my number?" We all laughed, but I knew they believed a *number* was already carved into their bone the day they were born. I told them my *number* was whatever I wanted it to be, that it was all up to me. They thought I was arrogant.

Bad things happened, but I wanted to believe that personal efforts played an essential role in my life. As I tried to fix the situation with the music professor, I put serious thought into embracing an opportunity to meet the guy. I wanted to give him, and more importantly *myself*, a chance. I had no clue what would become of it, but felt incredible and liberated at the thought that I changed my own perception to take control of my life and orchestrated events to steer its course.

* * *

"What do you study?" the music professor asked me at the next gathering when we had a chance to talk.

"History," I answered.

"Interesting!"

"What did you mean?" I quizzed him thinking he was being nice the American way. Well, Americans are very generous with compliments and pleasantries, and the Vietnamese are not. I was new in America and not yet comfortable responding to pleasantries from the Americans let alone a 'Vietnamese.' I expected the latter to spare me the social sweetener. The constant comparison and contrast at work in my mind often made me scrutinize people and things to my own disadvantage, maybe, yet I couldn't help it. On top of that, ever since I had come to the U.S., I often encountered Vietnamese Americans who rolled their eyes on hearing "history" instead of the familiar medicine, pharmacy, dentistry, or computer science as a subject of study. They could not see "history" and "money" together in the same string attached to a career to make a living. I know financial stability is foremost on their minds but don't share the same belief.

"Well, I believe people in arts or social sciences are interesting," the music professor said. "Maybe an artist myself I am biased, but I like history very much. There are many things in human history that fascinate me. Besides, most Vietnamese I have met study medicine or computer science. It is very rare to find someone who studies something else. That's why I think it is interesting that you study history."

I found his response true and honest. We talked. He appeared to be straight-forward, very opinionated, a positive and cheerful person. His artist name is P.Q. Phan.

A few months later, we started dating.

One of the early topics we covered was the nature of a romantic relationship. P.Q. told me that when he was in a relationship, his girlfriend or his wife became his first priority, not his parents. I was shocked at his honesty, and thrilled at the same time, because in Vietnamese culture, this is a sensitive issue. Up to this very moment, many Vietnamese still cannot make a choice between their girlfriend or boyfriend, or even wife or husband, and their parents. So heavily brainwashed by the Confucius teaching that one had an insurmountable debt to their parents, many Vietnamese automatically put love secondary to filial duty, as they were taught to do for so long.

I had been so many times aggrieved seeing how Vietnamese life was pulled backward just because the old and conservative reign over the young and control our society. It was painful and horrifying to see individual rights repressed and no social progress made. I also thought about how backward human beings were these days to still have to fight the same battles our ancestors did, especially when many came out victorious and we refused to follow their lead! Take the example of the "Self-Strengthening Literary Group" founded in Vietnam in 1932 by writers and novelists Nhất Linh and Khái Hưng. Almost a hundred years ago, they already deplored the outdated feudalistic values that turned women into third- or fourth-class citizens. They demonized monstrous mothers-in-law who wedged themselves between their son and his wife.

More fascinating was the story of Hồ Xuân Hương, an eighteenth-century poet with whom most Vietnamese are familiar and love still. She attacked male authority and fought for freedom in love and equality. A large part of her poems are double entendres. Hiding in her marvels at nature are carnal images and sexual meanings. Her poetry radiates a kind of palpable energy that serves as an outcry for those basic human rights already claimed by men all this time and that women are bereft of.

If only we learned from those pioneers! As I was growing up, I saw with my own eyes men around me choosing their parents and ignoring their wife and their children, or boys who chose their parents over their girlfriends. Relationship is broken and family life twisted just because people followed outdated traditions. It made me angry and sad.

I molded a mission for myself never to fall back into living life according to those condemning Confucius principles. If a man was not strong enough to stand by his wife, such a man was useless and not worth my time, I decided long ago. All this meant that I was willing to fight against tradition. In a relationship, as my husband was the one with whom I would share the rest of my life, not my parents, he should be my number one priority. As simple as that. Yet, frankly speaking, never before had I had a chance to say all those things out loud, thinking people would ostracize me for being 'rootless.' They already thought I was arrogant to take control of my life. I had lived my beliefs in silence. Until now.

In response to P.Q's question, "What do you think about that?"—that, without kids, a spouse being the first priority in a marriage, I told my date: "I believe in the same thing."

We became very good friends.

By the way, I found out later that the music professor did not possess a light pink shirt. It was more a salmon color. "I never like wearing that shirt!" he told me.

10. MISERABLE

JOINING THE PHD PROGRAM IN history at Indiana University was another dream come true for me. I was very emotionally cocky by this time, totally believing in my supreme capacity to cross cultures and feeling culturally invincible like a twenty-year-old.

I arrived in Bloomington on the summer afternoon of 2003. It must have been raining a lot the day before because the trees were still wet. They looked so fresh and green their lustrous color seemingly transported me back home to Vietnam. I did not associate this green with America before—the greenness from a mass of trees and not from a newly-cut lawn, a close-up greenness that hugged and wove around houses and along dirt paths to create an intimate atmosphere, at the same time warm and vulnerable.

When I got near Bloomington, the roads became so winding and hilly it reminded me of Đà Lạt. I was absorbed in the new yet familiar topography of the strange land. I was up and down and curved around the hills. The drive was so smooth like I was on top of the hill sliding a gentle waterfall into a dreamy river. I felt strange to develop an attachment to Bloomington landscape as if this could be another home away from home for me.

* * *

Right before I came to Bloomington, a white American friend L. told me she was glad I had an opportunity to experience a small university like BYU, and then a big university, Indiana University. I had no idea what she meant. Provo is a university city with a population of 115,000 and student enrollment at 34,000. Bloomington is also a university city whose population is 80,000 and student enrollment at 36,000 when I came—45,000 now. Why BYU was 'a small university' and IU Bloomington 'a big one' escaped my understanding at first. So did the differences between private and public university. But it soon became clearer to me what my friend meant.

The IU Bloomington campus is one of the top five most beautiful in the country. Limestone buildings dominate the whole campus. Red brick interface stands out and adds charm to the environment. With many lakes around and a lusty green in Bloomington, the buildings nestle among the woods and the hills and the creeks. Sample Gates, the main entrance to the university, is framed by two stone pillars in Gothic design each abutting an archway and ending with a low wall. It intermingles into the surroundings seamlessly as it faces Kirkwood Avenue that runs straight for blocks, shooting through downtown to as far as the eye could see. Even the fierce afternoon sun in Winter could not bend the view of the straight avenue dotted on both sides with a row of maples that turn red and yellow in Fall etching an archetypal image of Bloomington. Inside the gates, the little woods to the right with green leaves flying in the summer breeze were like a camouflage soothing my way into a wonderland. It was truly breath-taking.

This mesmerizing beauty, however, seemed to be interrupted by a pervasive lukewarm ambience here. The limestone buildings stood, beautiful, archaic and provoking. Inside of them, many dark corridors echoed with closed-door offices on both sides. The lack of glass windows and light makes everything and everywhere so quiet and gloomy. This ominous atmosphere stuck with me.

I arrived in Bloomington very early for the Fall semester. I got myself a carrel in the main library. It was a cubicle where I stored all the checked-out books, and my own space where I mulled things over in the years to come.

The department assigned me a mentor for my orientation in the program. It took several twists and turns before I could get hold of him. When it was time to meet, he showed up late.

You see, I have an issue with unpunctuality. When in Vietnam, I always went to appointments five to ten minutes early. Most Vietnamese people at the time did not appreciate this behavior. Living in a 'relaxed' culture I was supposed to take it easy and accepted that fifteen minutes late is normal. Well, I did not. I used to get really upset about that—I considered the people, the system and the culture messy. In response, people laughed at me.

In the U.S., I like the fact that people are punctual. It made me think that they did what they were supposed to do, and things happened the way they were supposed to. It was merely the surface, but at least life rolls smoother this way. By being on time we show mutual respect. I thought of it as an insinuation of scientific accuracy and efficiency where one second earlier or later makes a big difference in certain circumstances. So here I was, waiting for a mentor who was late and feeling completely pissed off.

When he came around and we started talking, there was such a distant manner in his voice and general expression that made me wonder why he bothered to be a mentor at all. I was already perplexed at the concept of a fellow mentor and this experience should not have been a big deal, except that I was still idealistic when it came to the U.S. Perfection was what I looked for. I found the opposite.

I don't remember the color of his hair, maybe black, neither the color of his eyes, maybe green. The Graduate Students Office where we met was a little too dark. Two chunky computers lay on the two tables sitting edge to edge. Everything was old. There were a few old wooden chairs, the type that swing and make the creaking sound at every turn. The chairs and tables were made of oak. Their light color un-shinny. The graduate students mailbox shelf to the left of the door unglamorous. It was one stale image of America that shocked me but I thought nothing about it then. The only American thing about this office was a note by the computer screen that said: "*I am not your mother, but you are welcome to clean up after yourself*" signed by the department graduate secretary. I liked the funny note that made me smile. The mother analogy sounded familiar, yet the note as a whole was so American. Something tasted like total freedom soaked every letter: We are free to display our sense of humor not only publicly but also officially. Only a friendly and open-minded American can think of implanting a serious business request in a funny note like this one.

I don't remember Vietnamese people smiling a lot growing up. Hard life stole our smiles a long, long, long, long time ago. In communist history, humor is like oil and communism water, in Vietnam. Anything official is managed and enforced by non-smiling, grumpy faces. Where there is totalitarianism there is no honest humor. Fear replaces everything as a common currency. The return of 'capitalism' changed everything. But more about that later.

The friendliness, positivity and humor in the note were refreshing. Ever since, every time I stopped by the office I recited the note in silence unwittingly triggering a friendly and cheerful white face to pop up in my mind. I appreciated the American sense of humor even when in reality a positive face was not in sight.

On that day when I came to the office, I sat on the oak chair facing the only window in the room and the mentor on the couch against the wall. In semi-darkness, I saw his face, not round and rather long, with a chin a little pointed. He was not a regular big tall American guy. Slender and small-built, he struck me as a gentle person. Maybe he was all that and kind. All I remember is his slow somber voice and lukewarm manner.

I never talked to the guy again and started shielding up in a heavy way.

* * *

My major was American history with a concentration on the Vietnam War, and my minor American Studies. Going to the very first class in American Studies, I was excited to find out what a big-school classroom was like.

More than an hour passed and there was a blank. I could not make heads or tails out of the professor's monologue, as if she was talking in code. She sewed her vocabularies along imperialism, post-imperialism, post-modernism into a quilt that looked like a most incoherent and tasteless one. I looked around the room, other students leaned back, unusually quiet and removed. I waited to see if anyone would ask a question. Nobody did. I was confused about the introduction into this class. The whole time I was trying to figure out, but failed, how I could weave Vietnamese culture into the strange threads of information to make anything out of it. The excitement of coming to class traded place right away with the frustration on leaving it. Almost immediately, I began to question my ability, and whether this program was right for me. Most significantly, I was stupefied and devastated by the imminent sign of plummeting confidence that I sensed was coming my way.

Walking down the cement stairs outside the building, I caught sight of an American Caucasian guy in the same class. I hurried up to him.

"Excuse me! Hi, could I ask you a question?" We had met at the department orientation earlier.

"Sure. What is it?" he replied. His look was rather stern and his voice brusque, though not totally unfriendly. I knew right then I was asking for trouble. But it was too late to pull away.

"What do you think about the discussion today? Honestly, I was confused. I hope you don't mind sharing your thoughts."

"You know, I thought the class was a little strange, too. I had no idea what was going on, either," he said non-smiling and looking a little annoyed. I did not understand why he behaved like that. And I thought all Americans were friendly.

"Do you really think so? I noticed that most of the students were so quiet, which is unusual." By now I tried to end the conversation quickly.

"Yeah. I believed many others felt the same way. Hopefully it gets better." He shrugged his shoulders.

"I hope so, too." I responded and we parted ways.

For that whole less than a minute exchange, he was courteous but I sensed the cold flare, again, as if I was talking to a corpse that could talk. As if he was saying if there was a problem then I was supposed to deal with it myself, like he was going to deal with it himself without the need for an exchange like this one. I was a little shocked and disappointed, not expecting this kind of unfriendly behavior in white people and in academia. Maybe being myself, direct and friendly, did not seem to be a smart strategy here anymore.

I started to think about America differently. *This* must be what my friend meant by IU being a big university, a public one with a more impersonal environment compared to BYU. In the back of my mind I realized that *this* was a realistic version of America, not the one I experienced at BYU. The same coldness that Vietnamese immigrants recounted about America that I heard when in Vietnam. This reality was often ignored by those seeking to come to America, like myself. This should be evidence again that white Americans were full of flaws, that not everyone would do the right thing, and that, most of all, America was not paradise as I expected.

Too stubborn to take the new reality into consideration, I leaned even harder on the belief that white Americans were friendly, open and happy.

For the rest of the semester, the students were very quiet in the American Studies class. I felt strange that nothing happened till the end, no solution to anything. Only then did it occur to me that the shining veneer on American society that I kept in mind had started to crack. I thought efficiency and problem-solving are key ingredients of American life. I used to think that every single American professor was perfect. What could I say, brainwashing was a powerful tool. In Vietnam, that is all we got: everything coming from America was shiny and impeccable. I did not meet any *Việt Kiều* who knew better. Neither did I encounter anyone who failed to praise the Almighty America. I also lived in Sài Gòn and around the Southerners. The more bitter they were, as belonging to the losing side, about the communist government, the more they clung to the American dream, e.g. going to America is a dream.

Those accumulations of skewed narratives were all my tattletale on the U.S. of A. My real experience now at IU proved to be different, I realized that. Unfortunately, I did not have the mental clarity at the time to form a constructive criticism, the sort that should have helped divert me from my superlative view of America towards a more realistic adjustment to the new terrain. I still believed the mishaps were trivial things I could overcome to achieve my academic dream in the American paradise.

Many years later I met an old friend who also took the American Studies class. She told me she had no clue what was going on in it and felt so dumb. "I looked at you and others in class and thought how smart you guys were," she said. If only we had talked to each other then!

A few months into the program, my encounters with people around me were not going anywhere. Something was missing and I did not know what it was. Something about this place that bothered me and that thing did not go away over time.

On a good day when I suddenly had a clearer vision of it, I began to think that people here were friendly but seemed unhappy. *They were supposed to be happy but they were not. How was I going to solve this piece of a puzzle?* I did not know. They were somber and so concentrated on their work making me think that I must muscle up to create an impression. And unless I could show them anything short of that muscular image of myself, it would not matter who or what I was. I began to worry. I did not know how to do it.

Except for the American Studies class, all other classes were fantastic. I enjoyed the class discussions even with my minimal participation. I loved the dynamics in a classroom where the professor and the graduate students were head to head in tackling issues of life. It was everything I thought graduate education was about, where people of equal intellect put in motion a search for truth. I also loved the undergraduate classes that I graded. I envied the American undergraduate students a superior education whose main purpose was to provide them with information and skills in order to help them *think* for themselves and make *their* own choices in life. All in all, almost everything was exactly what I looked for in an excellent education that we lacked in Vietnam.

Along the way, the pleasure of discovering incredible things about American culture and history and learning how things worked in academia and here in the U.S. was always outweighed by the grave concern that I did not know what to do with all the information. Neither did I see how I or my country fit in the larger picture of a better future.

* * *

I spent a lot of time in the library like other graduate students. I would sit there with a book in front of me. An hour later, I seemed to wake up and realized that I was still on the first page. *What was I doing all that time?*

In my library cubicle, I tried to zoom in on the one-hour blackout to find out what was going on. After much effort, I came to the conclusion that the standard procedure would be something like this: After reading a few lines of the introduction, I started arguing with the author. "I don't understand why you are whining about the Vietnam War here in the U.S. More than three million Vietnamese including civilians—a large part of them women and children—died by the end of the war, whereas 58,000 Americans died. Death by itself is a great loss and an irreversible tragedy. 58,000 is definitely an astronomical number, enough to create unfathomable sorrow for those left behind. Three million is unspeakable pain beyond imagination. Every single death is equally devastating. To mourn for fifty-eight thousand American deaths at the same time ignoring or belittling the three million Vietnamese deaths is not natural by any means. Neither is it in order with life. To hold an American life more valuable than a Vietnamese life, or any other life for that matter, is greatly disturbing to me. And blah blah blah."

All of these comments were in English. Then I turned to an imagined audience of friends in Vietnam and went: "Do you know that American soldiers looked at us in pretty much the same way they looked at the native Indians? That is how they fired indiscriminatingly at us just for the body count during the war. Do you know that the amount of bombs dropped in Vietnam during the war was more than the combined amount used in both WWI and WWII in the whole world? What rights do they have to just march in and kill us? And look at what you are doing? Nineteenth-century French romanticism! What a joke! What you need to do now is to stop digging up the past, and do something more useful. Create something new." These notes were in Vietnamese.

To be frank, the blackout, in the form of daydreaming, happened at BYU, too. Back then, cultural understanding started with people. I had my professor-mentors to consult with—I often flooded I.G.'s and N.Y.'s office hours with a tsunami of questions—and lots of good friends to hang around with. My whole journey of adventures in the U.S. began on the surface with classes at BYU; underneath it, the main processes of life-discovery and self-discovery continued to grow as our conversations widened in depth and scope.

The threads of discovery that I had started weaving in Vietnam formed their own patterns, now crisscrossing with newly formed patterns created from new threads extracting from the new people I encountered and inspirations, observations and reflections I had in the new land. The mutual understanding and respect I received from these experiences made disturbing facts I came across in the books become obscure and insignificant to me. In other words, I felt that I received enough goodness in people around me to sideline the horrifying facts in books. I was able to focus on the task at hand of studying, made possible and pleasant by supportive people around me. The episodes of daydreaming were out of excitement about future plans and changes that I wanted to see in my home country.

Here at IU, my whole attention already shifted to the negative mode. Disappointment in people around and doubt about myself made the blackout intense and destructive. It was a very common scenario that I played out again and again in my mind, everyday, every time I read a book, every time I saw something happen around campus that was stirring to me, every time I had a strange encounter with somebody which involved my clearing some misconception about Vietnamese culture. The commentary changed according to the topic of the book and the context of each circumstance. Mostly they involved American foreign policies, American encounters with Asians, or cultural biases of some sort.

One book after the next, one encounter after another, I grew desperate and furious seeing how imperialistic thinking played out, how dominant it was and still is, and how hopeless the situation of Vietnam was and still is.

I kept thinking about how true it was that the very thing that gave us pleasure also caused us pain. It is a duality of life. Nothing new about it, yet it never stops to unhinge me every time. I used to love the fact that through history I learned about how the world swayed. Now it was also via history that I learned about the most cruel political scheming that shattered peace and gushed down destruction and death on earth. In my dream, I came to the U.S. to learn about how the governance of a great civilization in human history has transformed human relations breaking down racial and social barricades to give us paradise on earth. I imagined mutual cultural understanding to be a standard of communication. In reality, in the new land, I belonged to a minority group occupying space designated by white Americans. And my country was an under-developed one invisible to the world. With still very limited knowledge about world politics I could not understand how this was possible in the twenty-first century. And we have the UN, NATO, WTO, the Hague, etc. America was supposed to be perfect, and it is not. I did not know how to handle this truth.

Fury and pain, I felt. I could not control them. More fury and more pain built up in me. Cell after cell. Until they took over my whole body.

As a Vietnamese citizen, I felt small and helpless. Vietnam as a country was present on the world map but hardly anyone saw it and knew of it. How was I to deal with that, with the fact that my presence here meant nothing, neither did my country to the world? It did not make sense at all.

The rage and the pain were relentless. They shrouded my mind. Until darkness became my eyesight and the sensation I felt. I could not think of anything to do to make it better.

Once in darkness, I lost out to clarity and critical thinking.

I forgot all the good things that happened to me earlier in the U.S.

My only thought remained: *how naïve it is for me to have believed in globalization, democracy, in justice and equality.*

Just like that, by the second year, I started having 'problems' at school and soon lost track of what I was doing here. I could only stay awake and remain focused for a few hours a day, mostly in the classroom. The rest of the time I was in an almost dozed-off state of mind. I was so sluggish I struggled hard to get anything done. The black-out incidents occurred more and more often. An hour and a half stretched to two. Sometimes I had to wake myself up to lucidity so many times in the afternoon I gave up on the reading and went home for supper.

The more time I spent with my imagined audience, the more cut off I was socially and the more lost I became. I did not know how to interact with my peers, the professors, and what to talk about. I was full of skepticism and doubt about myself, about people around me, and the whole world, all the time.

Did I mention I was socially awkward? One time I had a presentation in class. A couple of hours earlier I had a doctor appointment for allergy test. Something new I acquired after living in the U.S. for more than four years was seasonal allergy. I did not know it was a long and tiring test. The nurse injected two dozen types of allergens under my skin and made me wait for the reactions. Two hours later, I walked out of the doctor's office, suddenly feeling extremely depressed and lonely. Totally alone in this land. Nobody in Vietnam could understand. They would never believe the bad experience I had in 'paradise.' Neither would anybody here find my experience of any relevance to their life. Everybody was cocooned in their own world. So was I. I could end up being alone like this for the rest of my life, I suddenly thought out loud. I remember the warning about a lonely life in the U.S. before coming here. This must be it.

The crushing thought broke me. My legs were shaking. It was five thirty in the afternoon, just enough time to get to my six-o'clock class. Feeling exhausted, I decided to skip it. I went straight home without calling or emailing to let my professor know that I could not make it. And I did not feel a thing. It did not even occur to me that I should have done that. My mind was completely blank. In fact I had been operating on empty for a while. Only years later did I come back to my senses and gradually recall some of these incidents and feel horrible about myself. But at the time, I forgot all about it.

The following week I showed up in class as if nothing happened, and in my mind, nothing happened. Nobody mentioned the previous week at all.

And I never had school problems before. I was basically a trouble-free child as far as school was concerned. Now dragging along in the history program, in spite of all that I felt, I did not know exactly what the problem was. I felt like I was in a maze sandwiched in a line of people and pushed by those in the front and the back of me to move my feet one step at a time towards whichever direction the line was heading. My view was narrowed down to the neck of the person in front of me. Blind to the rest and partially paralyzed. I had been reduced to limping along. The thought that America failed me was still taboo. *No way. America is paradise*, I continued to tell myself.

When not in denial, I tried to find answers elsewhere. I went on the internet and checked my symptoms against the diagnosis of depression. Now, I did not know what depression was when in Vietnam. Post-war Vietnam was a bleak scene. We directed our time and energy on getting by. Even if we experienced depression, we didn't know it. There weren't a definition of, ways to detect and solutions to a non existent problem. Depression as a common concept and recognized as a mental condition to research and be treated appeared much later. That's when I had already left the country. For me now at IU, after a few years living in the U.S., the ominous presence of depression in people around me, via ads on TV and on the internet, had sneaked into my head. It stayed hidden and when needed popped up to serve as a ready-made problem. It was the last thing I considered but I could not resist its availability. So I thought I might as well check it.

Most of my symptoms matched. I ended up assuming I had chronic depression. It was neither good news nor something on which I was sold, but I felt a tiny bit better thinking I had something else besides myself to blame for all my problems.

Looking back, I realized that numerous little incidents happened. They had provided me with signs of reality in America that I ignored, all because I knew to accept them was to display a galactic betrayal, firstly, to my idealism of a paradise on earth—America, and secondly, to my aspiration of a glorious academic American dream—an ultimate ancestral dream that I built up for twenty years. (I will talk about this later.) It meant announcing death to them both. That is why I went through the whole process of mourning my own life-death, alive.

I blamed myself mostly. I was unable to figure out one thing that meant the most to me in this academic pursuit. Whatever I was reading and studying meant so little when I could not see my part in it. I could not see myself researching American history. I did not want to have anything to do with the Vietnam War. I did not want to become a professor.

What should I do to change the dominant American perception of the Vietnamese? What could I do to make Vietnam visible? I had no idea. Changing my major in the program at this point was impossible. Transferring to another university in this state of mind was unrealistic. Quitting was a dishonor and a disgrace to me and to my family. I did not even know what I was searching for. I kept thinking my current nightmare must be similar to the kind of identity crisis that happened to kids at twenty that I did not go through back then. If we are supposed to experience this at least once in our life, then it must have been happening to me now, fifteen years late.

As I raced to finish the course work at the end of the third year, I was faced with a decision to keep going or to quit. I knew I was in a free fall but did not think I had hit bottom yet. Very often, my mind was blank and I knew I could not go on like this much longer. Expecting all hell to break loose, and life to catch up with me, I hung on the only thing I knew for sure: I did not want to become an unhappy person like many I saw around me.

* * *

"Why are you doing something that makes you so miserable?" my good friend P.Q. asked me one day. He said it in a kind of if-you-have-a-problem-then-you-find-a-way-to-solve-it tone and attitude. "I don't understand why you choose to live your life this way."

I was used to his honesty and straight-forwardness, but I was taken aback hearing this. Every time we talked he surprised me with the American problem solving skills that I already admired in American people. Its practical spirit often reminded me of the beauty in the basic principle of logical thinking: if you have a problem, accept it and take one small action. Buried deep in a shit hole like I was, P.Q.'s comment was exactly what I needed for a reminder. In a tick of a second, a peck of hope was kindled in me: my problem was quite solvable.

At this very same second, there was another parallel process already going on in my mind.

Miserable? This word struck me first and hard. With everything that I went through, it never occurred to me that I was miserable. The funny thing is, the Vietnamese word for miserable is *khổ*—this Vietnamese word did not register with me. It was not in my vocabulary when my mission in life was to be happy. *Khổ*—I never owned it to disown it; I never took it up to abandon it now. I had chosen to live without it ever since I could remember. So if someone had ever asked me: "Why are you doing something that makes you so miserable?" in Vietnamese, I would have denied it right away, because whatever I was doing, no matter how hard it was, it was not *khổ*.

Yet, the sound of *miserable* soaked into my skin immediately. It is one word that the meaning and the sound in English match perfectly in my ears, not like words such as *commiserate*, *efficacious* or *egregious* whose meanings and sounds do not pair well in my mind. When I heard the word *miserable*, I felt, I smelled, I saw, I tasted the drag of pain and sorrow along its enunciation trail. I understood *miserable* as if it was a modified DNA in my body. I cannot explain why. Epiphanies work in mysterious ways, I guess.

On hearing the question, as if shocked by electricity, as if I fell off the cloud flat on my face, to use the Vietnamese analogies, for the first time in three years, I saw a glimpse of light somewhere down the abyss. It was true that I *was miserable*. I saw it now. I admitted to myself that there was something really wrong going on in my life at this moment and I needed to stop it. Whatever I wanted to do, I could not accomplish it in this state of mind.

It was like having pounds of ulcers removed from my body. I felt light and I could breathe again.

The duality of my thoughts-beliefs and my experience of reality now crashed into one.

I was ready to admit that the dream had been crushed, that America was not a paradise any more than Vietnam was a perfect nation on earth.

The disappointment in America made me reassess Vietnam in terms of what it meant to me.

And even though I recognized with horror that I did not know how to deal with this new reality just yet, I found peace knowing there was plenty of time to figure it out. The most important thing was to stop the free fall.

As I prioritized my well-being, I remembered choosing happiness and meaning. Studying U.S. history did not bring me those. I even felt silly to have imposed upon myself such a pretentious ambition of representing my country to spread mutual understanding. I accepted now to relinquish this role as a once obdurate determination that occupied my mind for years.

The abyss quickly turned into a tunnel. It was time I got out.

I quit the PhD program in American history.

11. GRANDMA

IN EARLY 1950, GRANDMA CAM took her two daughters and a son through jungles to reunite with grandfather Tín. The family settled down in Bồng Sơn village in Bình Định province. Bồng Sơn is the land of jackfruit and coconut in the central part of Vietnam. The typical living arrangement here is a small house on a piece of land that includes a small farm and a fruit garden. People also had access to the field which is a bigger area of land further from home and on higher ground. They divided their time and crop planting between the farm and the field. And everybody had jackfruit and coconut trees in their yard. On the sandy and salty soil, the trees grow and produce fruits without any tending. That is to say the average daily temperature there is above 80 degrees Fahrenheit. It also rains a lot, more than thirty-nine inches a year. The sun is abundant all year round.

Everyday meal for the family was a variation of the three items including rice, jackfruit and coconut, prepared with some degree of creativity. In the field, jackfruit fell on the ground like fallen leaves. People did not bother to pick them. For family consumption, they stepped into the garden. This ginormous fruit has green coarse skin and contrastingly sweet aromatic golden meat inside. Grandma Cam picked the young jackfruit. Raw like this, its inside is chalky white and inedible. She cut the thick skin away, boiled the inside then sliced it to make vegetable soup. The yellow sweet flesh of ripe jackfruit was a delicious dessert. Grandma Cam stir-fried it with fish sauce as a main dish. Jackfruit seed gathered from the ripe jack is starchy like potato. She mixed it in with rice. With coconut, she chose a mature one with thick and firm meat. Grandma cut the white flavorful fleshy kernel and simmered it as another main dish.

Everything was very savory the first week or two. After that, the saturation of colors and flavors as well as the familiar consistency of jackfruit and coconut dulled the taste buds. The sight and smell of them became more and more a haunting nightmare kind of food to the children.

Grandma Cam had an idea. She separated the meat of the ripe jackfruit and layered it with salt in a jar to pickle. The pot of mixture was left basking in the sun for months. In the end, grandma collected a kind of distilled liquid known to her family as jackfruit fish sauce to be used as a replacement for the regular fish sauce. My mom said it was very fragrant and tasty.

Everywhere, tons of coconuts sat in the yard. Day after day, people picked the green-shelled skull-shaped fruits that fell on the ground and piled them up like a monument. Transportation at wartime was disrupted making it hard to sell them. People could not drink all the juice even if they wanted to. To salvage what they could, they cracked the coconuts, scooped the meat out and pressed it to make coconut oil. The juice, they poured it on the ground or onto one another for a play shower.

During this time, grandfather also brought home some printing jobs for grandma to do for extra income. The simple life in Bồng Sơn lasted for a few months. Then grandfather moved the family to his hometown of Phú Long, also in Bình Định. Twelve miles away from Bồng Sơn, Phú Long was another liberated town void of any French presence during that time.

Cam's brother-in-law gave the family a piece of land. To be self-sufficient, Cam began to learn farming. She picked up the shovel and the hoe. She cultivated rice. She plowed the soil and sowed the seeds. When the seedlings grew to about a foot in height, she hired a helper to space them out.

Phú Long was a small village. Everybody knew everybody else. When it was time to thin out the seedlings, all adults in the village were in the field working. So were the children, to hang out and to 'help.' My mom and aunt Hương rolled up their pants to the knee and stepped into the muddy field inches deep in water. In the scorching sun, they bent over, dipped their hand in the water, and planted the seedlings into the soft soil. It was all fun in the beginning for the children, until my mom suddenly felt something moving around her leg. She quickly jumped back onto higher ground. It was a sticking leach. She pulled it with her fingers, it stretched. She let it go, it bounced back on her skin. "Mom! Something is sucking me!" she screamed. Everybody laughed on hearing it. Grandma Cam stepped on the bank and walked toward her. From her pocket she pulled out a small bag of lime and chili pepper paste. "Spread this substance around the mouth of the leach, *con*," she instructed. "It will fall off." My mom did. And the leach fell off almost immediately. No wonder there was a saying in Vietnamese that went: "Like a leach on lime," she thought out loud in her unpublished diary.

A year or so after the family reunion, grandfather lost his job. Aunt Hương said maybe because he was getting older—near 60—so the Việt Minh let him go. Grandma Cam then had to become a breadwinner. A peasant's life was tough, but Cam had to work hard to feed a family of five now including the three children, aunt Hương, my mom, and uncle Tuấn. They began going back to school.

On harvest day, all the adults in the village would start very early in the morning and stay up overnight to finish the milling. To the children nothing was more exciting than this event. They had a great time playing around hills of rice spitting out of the milling machines. Until it was too dark and they had to go back home for bed.

Using campfire light, the adults continued to push through the night till the work was done. By the time they had their rice in the baskets, the new day had begun. They were buried deep in the calculations. The year-end taxes revealed that after paying agricultural taxes with the harvested rice, there was not much left for

Cam's growing family. In 1952, grandma gave birth to the fourth child and the second son, my uncle Hùng.

"Sometimes, after a few drought seasons, crop production fell badly. Before your grandma even had a chance to put the rice baskets into storage, the Việt Minh already came and took them away," my mom recalled. "All the harvests were not enough to pay for taxes. There was no money to buy food and the family went hungry. I remember going to the rice field with your aunt Hương to try to catch the little shrimps or fish to supplement the daily nutrition. Most of the time we went home empty-handed."

The hunger did not subside. Grandma had to fall back on her last resort, the gold bracelet in her possession she had saved for a rainy day. She cut a chunk and sold it. Part of the money went to taxes. The rest to buy food for her starving children.

Then whenever starvation was lurking again at the front door, grandma cut another chunk from the bracelet. And another chunk. And another chunk.

Disappointed and desperate, grandma Cam took up silkworm rearing and silk reeling for extra income. Her children had new chores now. As older kids in the house, my mom and aunt Hương would be responsible for picking mulberry leaves to feed the silkworms. When these were tiny, they did not eat that much. A month or so later, they grew bigger and fed all day long. "I could hear the sound of the silkworms chewing the leaves away," my mom told me. That meant she and aunt Hương had to work harder to pick enough leaves to feed them. Every few hours the silkworms had to be fed. The work became so tiring, the kids had no fun at all. Lucky for them, it did not last long.

A short while after, grandma Cam stopped the silkworm rearing business. Maybe because it did not turn out well, my mom said. Grandma then turned to cotton planting instead.

"One morning," my mom recalled, "I woke up and saw your grandma in the middle of the house submerging in the mountain of white cotton balls that we harvested the days before. By her side sat the humongous spinning jenny that, together with the giant cloud of cotton balls, occupied more than half the living space. Grandma was spinning and weaving the cloth from the threads extracted from the magical cotton balls. She sat there working, and smiling."

A harsh life, but Cam was satisfied. It was not even a comparison to the stifling atmosphere in Huế where each of her moves was controlled by one rule or another. A mandarin's daughter had to do this and not that. Cam loathed it. On top of that, like everybody else, she had to deal with the French soldiers. Their presence on the streets was cause for horror and misery, as nobody knew when the rapes or the beating would occur.

Here in Bình Định, she was her own boss. She had her land and she worked it. She planted crops and made her own food, like everyone else. Aunt Hương told me: "I remembered nobody was too rich, neither were they poor. People were genuinely friendly and enthusiastic about life in the liberated zone. Everybody helped out one another and shared out of kindness. When the dates in the forest were ripe, the whole village woke up at three in the morning. From one end of the village to the other, people called out to one another. Taking their basket, they went in droves to pick dates. In the late afternoon, everybody returned carrying one large basket of dates. Local dates in Phú Long are small but sweet and flavorful. People consumed the fresh ones right away. The leftovers were dried, made into powder and saved for later use."

The children were also busy surviving and having fun in an age of innocence that transcended hunger and comfort. When the local berries, called *chim chim* and *dú dẻ*, began to give out fragrance that the children could smell a long ways off, they knew it was time to head towards the forest for berry picking.

That was life in Bình Định in the early 1950s and some of the work that grandma did. She considered this 5-year period the highlight of her life. From then on, she associated Bình Định with happiness.

* * *

When I visited aunt Hương in Đà Lạt in 2012, she showed me the picture of grandma Cam and grandfather taken on her first trip to Bình Định before she took the children with her on the second trip. Aunt Hương told me many times how much grandma Cam treasured that picture as it represented the happiest time of her life. I looked at the picture of grandma and grandpa. They were so young and beautiful, full of life. Aunt Hương also told me that, except for the Bình Định time, grandma was not happy at all in her marriage. She only endured it. That whatever happiness she gained was from her children. I felt revolted at this news as if I tasted bitterness at the thought that my grandma was unhappy. My memories of her are pure and perfect. When I was growing up in the eighties and building my childhood memories in Đà Lạt with her as a constant and sweet presence, I never heard a sad story from her. She was just as beautiful and sweet as a perfect grandma could be.

She was always working on something. I would hear her footsteps on the cement floor and that is how I knew where to find her. Bending over the basket of chayote leaves next to the low wooden cage, grandma Cam thrust both hands into the soft bundle of greens and pulled up two handfuls. She swung her body to the left and started sprinkling the leaves over the top openings of the cage. She was feeding the rabbits.

I came near to take a closer look at the animals. These cute and gentle creatures were chewing the leaves and looking at me at the same time. My favorites were the all-white one and the white one with black patches. I stared at the rabbits' eyes and imagined them as human eyes. "Their eyes are more beautiful than mine, grandma," I told her. "They are so big and round. This one has red color in the eyes which looks amazing." Grandma smiled. "The rabbit's eyes may be rounder, but yours reflect a deep soul, my dear." I felt sorry for the rabbits because, every time we came to visit grandma, rabbit meat was on the menu. It was grandma's treat for her hungry grandchildren from Sài Gòn.

Sometimes I found grandma in the kitchen peeling carrots to prepare the soup. Judging that she would be standing still for a while, I hung around and waited for her stories to pour out. She would show me the best way to handle things in the kitchen. Hold the knife in the handle, two inches away from the blade, she said. Keep your thumb right on the side of the handle, not on the upper or lower edge of the handle. I picked up a knife and tried it. Correct, she told me when seeing my fingers in the right position. Then she continued working. Then the names began to string along. Auntie Liên and grand uncle Ấm in Huế. Grand uncles Lai and Long. Aunt Kim Anh, uncle Hùng's wife. Grandma Quyên. Or Mr. Bòn who lived down the hill, on the terrace right underneath us, he was an undercover cop. Or the folk tales here and there which I recalled the least.

I came out of story time remembering few names, but many people. In her stories, people could be nice or nasty. And I chose to be the first. I wanted to do the right thing.

Đà Lạt was cool even in summer. The average temperature is around fifty-five degrees Fahrenheit. Grandma Cam always had a big shawl over her head that fell and covered part of her shoulder. Her gray hair tucked neatly under it. A loose sweater covered the rest of her body. Sometimes at night before going to bed, I saw her take off the shawl and let her hair hang. She combed her peppered hair. I remember being shocked at how long it was. It was really really long and probably became longer in the imagination of a ten-year-old, to the point it reached her knee.

Blackout was very normal in the eighties and happened every week. We would be disappointed if it occurred during the evening meal because somebody had to find their way in darkness to light the oil lamps. Other than that, once we finished dinner, blackout was even welcome. Remember that Đà Lạt is cool and electric fans were unheard of at the time, not like Sài Gòn where blackout equals no electric fans which is equivalent to heat, sweat and extreme discomfort. In Đà Lạt, "blackout simply means we do not have to use electricity and save some money," aunt Hương would say. We would hang out in the living room in the cozy semi-darkness of oil lamp and talk. We, the kids, often begged grandma to tell a ghost story. She told us funny stories as well. We laughed, we talked, and went to bed early.

In the large bedroom, several of us children slept in a queen-sized bed, cozy and happy under the fluffy comforter. In the other corner was grandma's twin bed. The tiny oil lamp glowed unevenly creating shades of darkness on the walls that would have normally twisted my young mind in mysterious way to make me see monstrous things; instead I saw grandma and her long white hair as a comforting presence that lulled me to sleep. On nights when the moon shined so brightly outside the window, grandma sitting and combing her long white hair framed a magical moment that engraved in my mind the sweetness of imagination, of grandma-ness, of an utmost innocent and happy childhood.

I could not help but think that grandma chose not to have her past interfere in the present so that her grandchildren had a prefect one. She never once yelled at any of us. She was always calm. The very character that hid in itself the unfolding secret of life source and wisdom that I could only gauge fully until hearing *the* following tale about her.

The fact is, as my mom and aunt Hương told me stories of grandma, they saved the most shocking one for last. By this time, I had already laid out all the chronological details on her life, ready to make a full sketch. The new story was so big it did not fit in. To make space for it, and to make sense of it, I had to shuffle my whole plan around.

Their story took me back to grandma's childhood, then to the tumultuous period of French colonialism in Vietnam at the end of WWII. It focused on the two years span right before grandma made the strenuous trip from Huế to Bình Định for the family reunion.

The revealing details from the story threw me over my head swinging like a needle among a huge bundle of rich fabric searching for a new thread to weave the story into the whole tapestry of grandma's life.

* * *

As the oldest daughter in the family, and the most gentle and clever, Cam was chosen by her parents to become a family caretaker. Her mother, my great-grandmother, wife of a mandarin, had to take care of a big and busy family, but not without help. There was a nanny, a cook, a gardener, and a rickshaw driver. Yet with ten children in total and twenty to thirty annual death anniversaries to organize, great-grandmother was still in need of somebody close to help her with the cooking and to take care of the children. The verdict came out that my grandma Cam would stay home and cook and clean and feed and bathe her siblings when they were young, and some more when they all went to school.

Cam really wanted to learn to read and write. With the help of one younger brother, Cam learned to do that. When her siblings brought home books from school, she would read every single one. When I was staying with her in the summers in Đà Lạt, she was as wise as a sage.

In 1946 after the coup to topple the Japanese administration in Vietnam, the Việt Minh liberated Huế. Not very long after that, the returning French soldiers pushed them out of the city. As this was happening, there was growing concern among civilians about the approaching violence. People in Huế were finding ways to take care of old people, children and women. They evacuated to safe areas they thought had no fighting. Grandma Cam was now married with three children and four months pregnant. With her husband stranded in Bình Định working for the Việt Minh, she moved back in with her parents. She and her sisters were then responsible for taking her half-paralyzed mother, her other young siblings and three children to Vĩnh Huế village in Triệu Phong ward, Quảng Trị province to avoid the fighting that might happen in Huế. Over there, her parents had built a very big house with a tile roof as an ancestral home. The oldest son of the family lived here with his family to take care of the tombs and the altars. In this big house made from teak, everybody waited out the fighting before they could go back to Huế.

During this time, Cam gave birth to a daughter she named Xuân Lan. Both my mom and aunt Hương remembered the baby had fair complexion and that she was beautiful.

For many months, Cam did not hear anything from her husband who had to remain in Bồng Sơn village in Bình Định to work for the Việt Minh. In the meantime, life continued in the big house in Quảng Trị. Everyone worked hard to try to make ends meet, tending the yard and the field.

"Everyday activities were also to watch out for warnings of coming raids. The French and Moroccan soldiers often came to search for Việt Minh," aunt Hương told me. "All the girls and women, on hearing the warning gongs, would hurry to smear their face and body with mud. It was said that this helped decrease the chance of them being noticed, e.g. raped, by the soldiers.

"One early morning, without hearing any gongs to warn us, everybody in the big house was suddenly roused up by the noise of foreign soldiers talking. They were already in the house. They made us go outside. When we stepped out, we saw everybody else in the village lining up in their yards. The soldiers rummaged through our houses.

"Two of us carried your paralyzed great-grandmother to the shade of the bamboo hedge on the side of the yard. She was sitting on the dirt ground holding a wooden box tight to her chest. The French soldier saw the box and asked her to give it. She refused. He reached out and tried to snatch it from her. Gripping the box with all her strength, great-grandmother was pulled forward by the sudden force, her upper body hanging in midair, her hands stretching and still holding tight to her asset. The solider was angry. He used the barrel of the short gun and hit her on the head. Great-grandmother's body thudded on the ground, her hands fell apart lifeless. She was knocked unconscious.

"When the French-speaking soldiers were done searching, they walked out, and set fire to the house.

"The whole village was on fire. Thatch-roof houses disappeared in minutes. More solid ones like that of your great-grandparents' took longer, but not long enough. After a while the hard-wood beams and poles, and even tiles, fell to the ground crashing. The heat wave was like a splash of hell fire sweeping over everybody's face. Everything surrounding us seemed to be engulfed in the fire and the heat. Then there was only the fire and the heat. Then the soldiers were gone.

"People came rushing and tried to put out the fire to save what was left. Great-grandfather's house became bare as a skeleton. The adults quickly made thatch roofs and walls to provide shelter from the rain and the heat.

"Everyone was exhausted and devastated, especially great-grandmother and grandma Cam. They both fell ill. During this time of distress, baby Xuân Lan became sick. She got a fever. Without medicine and doctor, the baby was dying quickly."

One day, aunt Hương saw grandma Cam sitting quietly, in the skeleton house, holding her dying baby tight. The tiny body became colder and colder until there was no breathing and no heat to feel anymore. Cam sobbed quietly.

The house was gone, the baby was dead. A very somber atmosphere set in the household. In 1947 they decided to come back to Huế.

More than a year later still not hearing anything from her husband, Cam took the three children to Bình Định to look for him.

Aunt Hương was six years old when baby Xuân Lan died. Death was not uncommon for children living in wartime. It could wreck her emotions and destroy her innocence. It could become a searing memory that haunts her in her dreams. Or it might not affect her at all. For someone growing up in peace, I could not claim to know or to understand how she felt at the time. What I saw in her face when she was telling me about the baby's death was a blank canvas. Her voice registered normalcy as if no emotions were supposed to be detected in it. My guess is that adults and parents don't talk about the death of a child. As if it is their own impalpable sin, one that makes their soul burn in hell for the crime they do not commit.

I did not hear grandma Cam mention baby Xuân Lan's death when I stayed with her in Đà Lạt. For the sake of her family, grandma moved ahead in life.

* * *

In 1955, after a couple of years out of work in Bình Định, grandfather got a job working for the new Ngô Đình Diệm regime established after the signing of the Geneva Treaty. He worked at the Representative Office of the Central Highlands located in Đà Lạt. So in 1956 he started moving his family from Bình Định to the new city. Grandma Cam was pregnant. It was Spring. Looking at the flowers along the roads, she thought to herself: "If I have a daughter, I would name her Anh Đào," aunt Hương recalled grandma saying so. Anh Đào means cherry flower. It seemed to me grandma found a break from war. The war continued, but at least in the new home she had her own version of R&R.

Đà Lạt during the first few years of the Ngô Đình Diệm government was quiet. In Cam's family some peace and stability set in. In 1957, Cam gave birth to her fifth and last child, my uncle Hoàng. So there were five children in total in grandma's house: aunt Hương, my mom, uncle Tuấn, uncle Hùng, and uncle Hoàng. They were growing up fast.

Grandpa worked and earned a good living. He shared, however, only a limited sum with grandma Cam, my mom told me. He used the rest to buy land all over Vietnam without his wife's knowledge. For a few years, he was a *quận trưởng*, similar, but not equivalent, to an American county superintendent, in Buôn Ma Thuột overseeing law and order of many towns. Aunt Hương guessed that he must have bought a lot of land there, too. That is to say Cam had to take care of a family of seven with a very tight budget. During this time, my mom and aunt Hương were getting ready to enter high school. Instead of staying in Đà Lạt they wanted to go to Huế because their uncles told them that the schools there were superior. In 1958, aunt Hương went to Huế. The next year, my mom followed. Three years later uncle Tuấn imitated his sisters and asked to go there as well. Grandma Cam said yes. She made all these opportunities possible to her children, whereas high schools in Đà Lạt were quite good and grandma Cam could have kept her children close by. With one baby son and one 6-year-old son, Cam settled in for a quiet life in Đà Lạt.

The calmness came to an end soon enough. As the raging war escalated, every Vietnamese, including her grown-up children, was caught in its clutches. Free choices she gave her children led them to the most disturbing places in life a war-wrecked country could possibly churn up. By 1973, her life was divided between her various visits to the prisons in Sài Gòn to see her first daughter, my aunt Hương, and the son-in-law, aunt Hương's husband; to the first son, uncle Tuấn, in another prison in Côn Đảo; and to uncle Hùng, her second son, in the frontline in Quảng Trị. Prison visit trips were so costly grandma decided to work to make up for it.

She opened a home store selling yogurt and various kinds of *chè*. At the time, because not many people knew how to make a variety of *chè* as she did, grandma's shop was doing very well. People all over Đà Lạt, including American soldiers, came to her shop everyday for her yogurt and chè.

Where was grandpa all this time? I am not sure. Whenever I asked about him, my mom, my aunt and uncles gave me only bits of information. When in Bồng Sơn and Phú Long, he was working and out all the time. When in Đà Lạt, he was working and went on field trips all the time. When in Buôn Ma Thuột, he was totally MIA. Since 1968, he had been working in Sài Gòn and did not return to Đà Lạt until 1972. That meant grandma was a single mom on and off. Grandpa was always busy working somewhere doing his own things, and hardly a presence in his children's life. Not even in his wife's. Grandma Cam had gone through life as a lone fighter.

By now, I am so used to the ups and downs in grandma Cam's life. They echo like a familiar tide that goes up and down with fascinating rhythms. They join forces with the tide of my life to create a monumental circle, one that I carved out of my mind to put on a canvas of time. Stroke by stroke, I collected memories for the picture. I highlighted the post-war tidal waves of hardship that hit the country hard following the end of the war in 1975. This is when grandma was the most real and closest to me. I could hear her and touch her then. She talked to me about the lands that grandfather acquired before 1975 without her knowledge, and that he lost all of them after 1975. With more caution, she, on the other hand, was able to hang on to the second property she bought during wartime from her yogurt-and-chè savings. "The lesson here was to trust your wife and treat her with respect," she once said. She also talked about how the family lost any money they had in the bank when the government changed hands. Within a few years in power, the new communist government organized several currency adjustments. It was a governmental strategy to make sure any well-off family from the old regime was stripped of their wealth to become equal to the rest of their egalitarian countrymen. The family was completely broke, like many others at the time.

Then the tide receded again in the late 1980s tailing the economic reforms. All her children, communists and non-communists alike, took a breather. They flourished again, and the number of grandchildren grew. Grandma Cam was a huge presence in all her grandchildren's lives. She came to Sài Gòn to see us when we were small. We visited her in Đà Lạt as we grew, in those memorable trips and vacations of our life.

* * *

I looked at the picture of happy grandma and grandpa in Bình Định again. They were young, beautiful and full of life. But now every time I looked at the picture I saw the teak house in Quảng Trị in flames and grandma Cam holding her dead baby. Her tears for the children, for herself, her people and her country crystalized into a huge knot of sorrow inside her. It consumed everything she had and was. Grandma could not even cry. It is from these experiences in life that the knots accumulated and bubbled up, then oozed out over the many years as deep lines on her face, as wrinkles on her hands, and invisible scars all over her body. I remember the deep lines on grandma's forehead. But on a second look at the picture, I see my grandma combing her magical white hair in the moonlight. I could not imagine how the gland system in our body works but it seems to me grandma's tears were flowing like the springs thrashing up and down and inside and out so violently they canceled themselves out, leaving the surface calm and peaceful. The wrinkles on her forehead ran like deep winding rivers that echo through the forest of her hair and turn her face into a picturesque timeless image.

Sometimes I heard my mom, my aunt and uncles talk about the pieces of land they could have had. Grandma never really knew how much land grandpa bought and exactly where. And she never cared. Some relatives and friends thought grandma made a big mistake by not caring. They said she should have demanded more financial responsibility from grandpa. They may be right about this. But to a mandarin's daughter like grandma Cam who sympathized with the Việt Minh, the Việt Cộng, and so progressive as to believe in true love and equality since young, any form of manipulation is considered low. Till the end of her life, she chose free will.

Grandma was born into supposed privilege. It was neither something to be proud nor ashamed of, because like most other Vietnamese in wartime, she suffered unbearable hardship and loss. But she chose not to whine. She always sang revolutionary and folk songs to put her children to sleep. While she was denied the freedom she desired, she vowed to make sure her children would have it. She didn't make my mom and aunt Hương learn to cook and clean. "My cooking and cleaning for dozens of years is enough to cover for you both in this lifetime," she told them. "All you need to do is to study and do something useful with your lives." She sent all the children to school wherever they wanted, to study whatever they wanted. She set them free to find true love in life.

I find it hard to understand the free spirit in grandma. A strong, stable, wise and free-spirited person like that sustains and refreshes life any where, any time. And the Vietnamese often think people like grandpa who went to school and learned to speak French or English hold the threads of life! Traditional thinking like that is so outdated. In my book, grandma Cam and people like her are the heroes. Ever since she rescinded her rebellion against her father's last wish, Cam fought the crucifying circumstances of war and death, and buried all her sorrows. She made things right for her children and grandchildren. For one who knew best what loss meant, she aimed for the future.

* * *

In 1986, the year Halley's comet was bursting past the earth on its way out, Đà Lạt was bitterly cold. Even the earthworms crawled up and tried to get into the house for some warmth. Old people died off one after another. Some died sitting, others eating, still others lying in bed during sleep. My grandfather died of a stroke.

"A few months after his death, I saw him in my dream," grandma told aunt Hương. "He came to me and asked me to go to Bình Định with him. But I said no."

Seven years after that, grandma passed. "A few months after her death, before the hundredth day, I dreamed of your grandpa and grandma walking together in a beautiful garden," aunt Hương told me. "Maybe they met each other again there. That beautiful garden could be *thiên đàng* or *địa đàng*." I am not quite sure what to make of this comment from aunt Hương. *Thiên đàng* means Heaven and *địa đàng* Paradise on Earth. Aunt Hương is a communist. Maybe she does not believe in Heaven, but paradise on earth is acceptable.

Either way, maybe grandma is happy now in the celestial garden with grandpa. Bình Định meant happiness to grandma. It was where they took the precious picture. She considered the five years in Bình Định the highlight of her life. Yet, she rejected grandpa's request in her dream while she was alive. Maybe she forgives grandfather now, maybe she accepts his love in whatever way he could express it, somewhere out there beyond this earthly life.

By accepting this scenario, I am seeking compromise with myself and accepting the traditional behaviors against which I have been fighting so hard all my life. *No, I am not accepting deep-seated, selfish behaviors as being the best one could offer for the one they love.* It is easy to compromise when it comes to aging and death. I want to settle a score in my mind imagining grandma to be happy with grandpa but I also know that she was uncompromising. As my fight for deserving happiness and justice in the twenty-first century entails, maybe she continues to fight for the kind of happiness she thinks she deserves somewhere beyond here. Having a date with grandpa in the beautiful garden may be one step forward to introducing him to a romantic way of courtship she wants him to follow.

I know which scenario is good for my soul. Yet, reconciliation is a journey most unexpected and personal. While building a life in America as a naturalized U.S. citizen, I am as unsure about the reconciliatory path grandma takes as I am uncertain about my own. Curiosity for life brought me to America. Love and happiness kept me here. After I quit the doctoral program, my confidence was at its lowest ebb. Waiting for a normal life to be happening, I knew the struggle to establish my path here went on no matter what, and I would move forward. I didn't know when and how.

One thing I keep in mind every step of the way: whatever I do, I aim for the future.

12. WEEDS

1980s—ONCE UPON A TIME, I grew up in a big city. Weeds were a rare spectacle. I also grew up in a traditional intellectual Vietnamese family, I would never have anything to do with weeds. *Aren't they associated with peasants?*

My ancestors were court mandarins. Words interlaced their background. Literally, they were in love with words, especially words on the pages, and more specifically words they had written with their own hands. *Our hands are not made for pulling weeds.*

* * *

THE COMMENCEMENT WAS SET FOR late May. My friends were excited about the robe and the ceremony. They were planning for the big day with fun that would last till after midnight. Me, I had already decided not to go. "Just a bachelor's degree," I thought. "What's the big deal?"

Eventually, my bachelor's degree didn't come in the mail. I picked it up at the administration office.

That's what happened twenty-five years ago.

I had a love-hate relationship with diplomas. In a way, it was mesmerizing and mysterious like my family's genealogy. Going on for more than eighteen generations, it included in its pages many tantalizing characters and stories, mandarins and concubines, soldiers and activists, rebels and orphans, tombs and ghosts, as well as innumerable mementoes, scrolls and reports, plagues and degrees. It generated in my mind a thick mixture of distance and closeness. Counting everything tangible and non-tangible, they created in me a simultaneous sense of fogginess and awe to the point of not knowing which part was real and which part mythic when it comes to me and a diploma.

The day I held the bachelor's degree in my hands, I remember thinking: "Is this *it*? That much work for a bachelor's degree! Nothing much at all." I felt as if I had learned nothing to earn this degree. For days, I kept thinking that something huge, not covered by this degree, was missing. Something real and raw as life itself.

The gnawing thought haunted me.

My early memories of life must have tasted great as my jaw dropped open many times when I witnessed, both first- and second-handedly, people around me live. My grand uncles walking through jungles for months to get to the liberation zone in the 1940s to join the Việt Minh; my aunts and great aunts hiding in the bunkers while a blanket of bombs was falling from the sky over their heads during the American War.

Or a street vendor outside my elementary school gate. His dark wrinkled face engraved awe in my young mind. He was completely different than the fair-skinned, well-dressed, and well-read people I was taught to consider as appropriate or noble—he scared me a little. At the same time, the liveliness in his facial expressions and the proficiency in each of his movements as he went about conducting his business captured my full attention. The faded hat over his head made his grinning brighter as he shouted out offerings for his colorful popsicles.

Or a happy smiling father who rode a moped to pick up his children from school. In his vehicle he stacked the smallest one in the front and three bigger ones in the back, their skinny legs dangling on the sides. As he drove away, I could hear their chatters fading in the afternoon sun.

Or a woman owner of a convenient stall in Phú Nhuận market who negotiated prices with my mom with assertiveness.

These images stimulated my nostrils with the real fragrance of life.

I just sat there and listened; stood there and watched.

Deep down, I wanted to scream in excitement, to sing, to dance, to jump around to celebrate life, but I could not. The Confucius teaching I had imbibed never said anything about acting out one's feelings. In fact, it does not allow raw feelings to exist. Everything was about control. While it provides instructions on how I should talk, smile, sit, or behave so that I could express my controlled feelings in appropriate Confucius ways, it represses impulsive physical reactions. So there I was, not being able to move a muscle. Those people represented full life, while I something immobile, old and dead. I had no idea what it is they held inside that allowed them to join the war in action, to smile and to talk freely, to be comfortable in their own skin, when I could not. But I liked to have what they had. I envied those people for what I called "the sense of action" in their lives and came to believe strongly that 'actions' were an ultimate way to live one's life, the only way I could grow to become who I wanted to be. I did not know then what I did later to resist Confucianism. I thought those people used to be deadbeat-Confucius like me before they became alive. So for me to transform, I had to go through the old and the dead to get to life. Then one day I could achieve something similar to their part of life.

Ever since, I have craved for the so-called 'actions.'

But I wanted an even better part than theirs. Assuming that I did not want to become a worker like them, I convinced myself the only way to acquire that kind of action-experience and to own those memories was to join the academic world starting with the bachelor's degree. As if with the ambivalence I wielded towards my background, the harder I worked against it the more I was drawn to it.

I began taking aim at the degrees with a rigorous belief that behind them were doors to actions and real life.

It turned out the part of life I wanted to taste from this bachelor's degree did not come along in the same package—*such a taunting bitch.* I felt so disappointed. The following days, I began occupying myself with thoughts about how to acquire all the degrees in the world. Maybe an undergraduate degree was not much, but a graduate degree would bring me what I was looking for. The educational path would lead me to the highest degree available, which translated to the best possible path to the most meaningful exuberant kind of life, to knowledge, truth, wisdom, life experience, and self-discovery—e.g. all the important things that represent the 'sense of action' for which I craved.

I poured all my energy into pursuing it.

After graduation I was teaching ESL, at the same time preparing myself for any study abroad opportunity that came my way.

As the twenty-first century was around the corner, predictions about the future aroused people. Would the world come to an end? What would the new century be like? Some wondered whether they should stock up on food supplies. Others were concerned about whether the computer screen would pop up problem-free the second the new century arrived. I thought people were secretly expecting something magical or earth-shaking to happen as the New Year's Eve countdown burst into cheers. I did. I celebrated the twenty-first century with news of my scholarship to attend Brigham Young University in Provo, Utah, to pursue a masters degree in American Studies.

* * *

I arrived in the U.S. in 2001 with two suitcases. Each one was filled up one third with books in both Vietnamese and English. Among them Faulkner's and Kim Định's took the most space. The truth is I had an obsession with the written word; as if any word on a page of a book was a golden one to swallow. Not just me, the whole culture was like that. We went about our everyday lives citing our favorite poets and authors and Confucius maxims like a religious enthusiast quoting the Bible. We sent cards to each other with messages embedded in stanzas from our favorite poems or quotes from Confucius. These actions were deemed poetic or even romantic. I might be a little bit more obsessive than others, mostly because I came from a family with a very long scholarly tradition. In its recent history, my grandfather was a teacher, my father a literature professor, and my mom a literature teacher and poet. I did not want to part with my books when flying to America, understandably. After finishing the master's program at Brigham Young University, I went on to Indiana University to pursue a doctoral degree, continuing to submerge myself in the world of books.

Along the journey I discovered new things about the written words.

It was 2004 in Bloomington, Indiana, around a dinner table with guests at my boyfriend's house. More than halfway through the meal, after we talked about music and school issues and travels and social events, my white American guests began to talk about their family, where they and their parents and grandparents were from, and all the incredible things they had done. Their stories enthralled me, and reminded me of 'the slices of actions' that I yearned for.

On my part, I had nothing to say about my family. Except for some ghost stories, I knew no details about my parents and their pasts. I knew a little about my country's history but didn't see myself in it. It's like I was living in a house full of beautiful objects and, when the tornadoes hit it, I found nothing around to cling to. I would be swept away and disappear in the storm without a trace. I was totally rootless in life. Compared to my guests, I reasoned, I did not gather enough memories and 'actions' to tell a good story the way they could. What was my story? What was my voice? I had none. To develop a voice to tell my story the way I wished and to use that voice to fight for something I believed in so that I achieved 'actions' and felt belong to this life, I needed an anchor to hold on to.

I did not find this voice nor that anchor in the PhD program in history. I had been burying myself in books, in the old and the dead, hoping to find a way to life. Around the dining table, I was facing real life and did not know how to handle it. "What does all this mean?" was a frantic question that chewed me up at night.

Torn to pieces and cornered throughout many midnight nightmares, I eventually shed ignorance and disillusion. Reading books, the way I did, was all wrong. Instead of challenging the outdated written words or established values, I glorified them and gave them more life than they deserved. Not trying and fighting to use my own words, I gave up my voice. It did not matter how many books I read, it was all about how I used them to develop skills to create something new, something I could call my own. Compared to the American people who I believed have good skills, critical thinking and creativity to build actions in life, I had been desperately clinging to the dead world of written words forgetting how to act alive. Such a crippled way to view and live life! Such a fallacy!

On that day when I could no longer make sense of the written words, and could also no longer find excuses to stay in the program to look for meaning, I quit the PhD studies.

I could not tell my parents I quit the program, only that I took a year off and would come back after the rest. Nobody in my circle of Vietnamese family and relatives and friends would understand why I quit the doctoral program. This was supposed to be my dream and one that many others in Vietnam might not be capable of achieving but who would look at it as a final door to the ultimate dream in life—a dream of forever success and happiness. I could not tell them I threw away such a mouth-watering dream.

I did not know what to do. At the same time I had the luxury of being at home doing nothing and being happy. Being married, in 2006, to the music professor at IU, I looked around Bloomington and was surprised to see many American women enjoying domestic life. They consider it a luxury. This is Bloomington culture. As a small university city, Bloomington has an exceptionally high percentage of a highly educated population. Everywhere I look, there are overqualified people doing low paid jobs. Many women and men come to town because their partners got jobs here and decide to stay at home raising their family. Others accept any kind of job they can get for an extra income and to keep busy. I could do the same and be happy either way. Except that growing up as the daughter of a generation of idealistic and fighting women, I expected sweat and blood from life. Something was missing in my life in Bloomington to make it a true paradise.

In my parents' time in the 60s not only were the war and civil rights protests and feminist movements popular in Vietnam but also the pressing demand of wartime reality could not be ignored. Everybody needed to do something to contribute and to survive, especially women in families where the men had gone into battle. Working hard was a virtue my grandparents and my parents nurtured.

By the time the war ended in 1975, more than three million Vietnamese had died and the country was torn to tatters. The disastrous effects dragged on as I was growing up in the 1980s. Hunger was a normal thing. It pushed everybody out of idleness and landed them on the same threshold of labor for survival. To keep one's family afloat, everybody had to try their hand at more than one job. My father was a professor of English at the University of Pedagogy in Hồ Chí Minh City and my mother a high school teacher at Nguyễn Thị Minh Khai. They both took on extra work to supplement their meager income. They taught evening classes for a while.

At some point, I also remember going to a local market on the weekend with my mom to sell liquid soap. It was an open-air market. There were only a few trees around and a ton of people scattering all over the dirt ground. Vendors and buyers were shoulder to shoulder and their exchanges bustling. The scorching sun was raging. The air was so thick it kept the voices bouncing back into one another like working bees in a hive.

People were making a living in whatever way they could. Sitting on the ground or a stool, squatting, kneeling, standing, they had wares in front of them ready for sale. Meat and fish, vegetables and pots and pans, clothes, shoes and so on. Some lucky vendors found refuge from the heat in the shade. When there was no more slice of shade to share, others had to make do in the sun. I looked around for a shady spot, in vain because we arrived late. Here, life and work were at the most basic level, and hard work mattered the most. I don't remember whether we did sell anything because I was too busy watching people.

Rations continued to be the way of life until 1986. By this time, hunger became our second nature and turned the craving sensation into a reinforcing quality of self-control. Or at least it was that way for me. During this time, coal was energy. My mom would buy a bag of coal and heave it home. Looking at the heavy bag, I cracked my brain trying to imagine how she would lift it up on her bicycle and pedal home. Inside the bag was a mixture of coal dust with rice husk or sawdust, and very soft mud. The four or five of us would sit around the opened bag and begin to make magic with our hands. My little brother and I would compete to see who was faster. Gloved with plastic bags for protection, I was able to produce in less than thirty seconds one big button of coal the size of my palm an inch and a half in thickness. He was not far behind. In the end, we shared the wins and loses. After a few days, the coal patties were dry and ready for use. No one in the house was spared the smoke when we layered the coal discs into the stove to burn and started cooking.

That was working as I know it. For me now to look back at those times, it is not hardship that I remember. The memories become endearing, like a painting that gave me fright at first but that over time, viewed from a different angle and under different lighting, morphs into a dreamy treasure. I would not trade them for anything. I learned very early the value of honest labor for survival.

Shoes. High heels, wedges, straps, platforms. In bright colors of red and blue and yellow and orange. That is how I remember the second half of the 1990s. It's like waking up from a dark grey nightmare to the rainbow morning sunlight. We would drive past the shoe store right outside the main street where we used to shop and headed towards the ones on Trần Quang Diệu street where the mecca for shoe lovers was located. The good smell of genuine leather and hand-made shoes at the old store was unable to compete with clusters of small shops displaying glittering colorful vinyl straps that one could see from a distance.

Welcome to globalization. The open market policy was at work for approximately ten years and began to take its own course of action. With rations down the drain, family businesses, mini hotels, joint venture and foreign companies, and flashy shops mushroomed. Personal aspirations interwoven with familial expectations and obligations pushed us to embrace various socio-economic opportunities that opened like never before. Teaching English as a Second Language became a hot job. I enjoyed the luxury of having more teaching job offers than I could possibly handle. Many people I knew worked around the clock, teaching at government institutions, private schools and for companies. They accumulated rigorously and turned a green page in their life. Vietnamese people had a real chance to work hard and made money with a vengeance.

Some economic freedom allowed the return of lifestyle and viewpoint diversity in Sài Gòn. By the time my generation graduated from college, we were full-fledged adults each having baggage we carried along matching the ideological background from each family. Opportunists, idealists and communists alike, we found our own spots in the new arena unrestrained by rules, regulations, or principles. With free choices, many of us found comfort in the old cocoon of traditions. Others broke loose to explore any piece of freedom they could get their hands on. And still others stood in the middle of the road. Regardless of which group we belonged to, as long as I can remember, the core of our self-esteem was work and independence.

The ideas about women's liberation were very popular, at least in a big city like Sài Gòn, as if they were oozing out of every corner. In the early part of our lives, the socialist education stressed gender equality. Post-war scarcity required contributions from everyone, making labor equality common sense and survival all the more weighted down on most families.

We Vietnamese women have also been conscious about our historical second-class status. It is only natural that we welcomed with open arms the feminist movements that we learned were happening around the globe in the 90s. The sense of female empowerment was pervasive. Young Vietnamese women talked a lot about the importance of being independent by working hard and making our own money—like Western women. We admired modern women who put off marriage until later. I had planned to put career above family life—like Western women. Many of us shared this same notion. So at the end of the century, everyone around me was working even harder than before, especially young career women. Working was the ethics of life. This I felt in the bones.

As I tried hard to relax in Bloomington, I knew I could not sell this little piece of paradise to others while I myself struggled reconciling 'not working.' Every time we were on the phone, my dad would ask me: "When are you going back to the PhD program?" This question popped up at the beginning and the end of our conversations. My mom was not that anxious but she was curious as well.

A few weeks turned into a few months, then a few years. The guilt and pain from quitting, and the devastating consequences they caused did not recede. The part-time jobs did not help, either. My family-and-friend circle would not understand me staying at home doing nothing or a part-time job which they considered a joke. Whenever I talked to some close friends and relatives on the phone, I could feel how hard they tried to hide their puzzlement.

Behind the "Oh, I am glad you are happy" or "It is good that you got a part-time job. The most important thing is that you are happy," I knew the thoughts running around their heads would be "How weird! Staying at home and doing nothing!" or "She is young and educated, why a part-time job?" The awkward pauses and their tone were revealing.

How I wished to have a break from family.

That said, quitting the PhD program and facing a 'jobless' life was a horrible reality I had to face. Deep down I did not like it at all. This lifestyle was also against my belief in the American sense of independence. Besides the financial element, I had to know what I wanted in life and pursued it.

I did not know what I wanted to do.

A lot of days I found solace from guilt and confusion in the loop of reminisces about my post college life in Vietnam. I jumped through all hoops trying to learn and relearn a way out of it, to break the clueless circle.

After college graduation, I took a hundred percent control of my life. When the internet and cell phones had just emerged with no capacity to present distractions yet, opportunities, problems and stress from free market competition were quite manageable. Students went to school because they genuinely wanted to learn something and to improve their lot. I loved my teaching job and my students. I became a popular ESL lecturer at the university. Asked to teach three classes, I would accept two. It was a reality in Vietnam then, and still is today, that lecturers and professors need to moonlight, legally actually, at semi-private colleges for extra income, to make ends meet for all and to make it rich for some. I would take two to three evening classes at those places, out of four to six classes I was asked to teach. I decided how much money to make to enjoy a comfortable life.

With total control and freedom, I planned to explore things I did not have a chance to do before, due to my very protective parents. Five mornings a week, I woke up at four and drove my scooter to the swimming pool in Tân Bình district. Determined to swim out in the ocean, I took two months to teach myself breaststroke and freestyle strokes.

My sister and I also went to Câu Lạc Bộ Phụ Nữ (the Women's Club) for a class in flower arrangement. This was the government-owned club where they organized all kinds of classes, from martial art, languages, to fine arts and everything else in between. Remember that 'google' was not a verb then and 'everything' people wanted to know about the world around them, including the how-to projects, was not available at their fingertips yet. So we learned a few things from this class.

Then I took a Chinese class because I liked drawing. Practicing writing Chinese would be like drawing, I thought. It turned out to be a boring and useless class. I dropped the silly idea after one class and took a real drawing class. I learned to draw an appetizing apple, a beautiful orange, a draping hat, and so on. Fun as it was, I was too restless to sit in meditation to pencil a plate of fruits on paper. Then I thought maybe oil painting using broader strokes would be more fulfilling and a faster route to accumulating 'actions.' Before venturing into that, to change the scene, I hired a coach to teach me and practice table tennis twice a week.

I also travelled. Sometimes alone. A train journey to Huế and Nha Trang, a boat trip to Mỹ Tho, a speedboat escapade to Long Hải, a group motorbike visit to Đồng Nai and the Mekong delta and beyond.

One thing at a time, I explored my life with strategic planning.

All those pleasures disappeared in America even when I had the luxury of time and resources.

I did not know what I wanted.

I missed the determination, the passion and the excitement in exploring myself and life.

In the windowless office of the survey center where I had my second part-time job, I did meet real Americans. Many of them were overqualified for the job just like me. They had real life issues. One black woman, S., tall and beautiful like a model, broke up with her boyfriend of many years and found herself a single mom with a teenage daughter. Another Caucasian guy, D., had a PhD-student girlfriend whose study had something to do with polygamy and sex slaves, as I learned from my brief conversation with him. S. told me: "You don't know the whole story. His girlfriend has a boyfriend already, and she allows D. to stay at her house, in the basement, as a sex slave for herself."

"What on earth are you talking about? Oh my God! Wow, how intriguing is that!" I gasped.

Then there was M. who was battling poverty and obesity. She and her husband lived in a trailer on the West side of town. She was not happy about her situation but accepted it with grace. And there was B., a very nice and sweet person. Half of the year, he and his business partner ran a log cabin rental facility around Monroe lake. The rest of the year he worked a part-time job, like this one at the survey center. He was adorable. I thought he was secretly gay.

In the office cubicle, sipping at my own life, my non-tangible problems instantly became so minuscule in comparison to my co-workers'. The survival matters they had to deal with seemed more realistic than mine. By now, I was past 35. After six years in the U.S., including two years exploring my new freedom with odd jobs, I started gaining some weight at the same time as gaining some insights into American life as an ordinary alien. Now that I was a part of it fighting to find my own niche, real life in America was not much different than real life in Vietnam. And yet, even though I was face to face with life, I concluded that this was not a slice of life that I imagined having in America. Like a sleeping beauty who woke up to a world not to her liking, I fell back to sleep. In my dream I gravitated towards a kiss of entitlement.

By the time I quit my third job, I was not sure whether I was chasing life or my own shadow, or both. I couldn't tell them apart. The pain from quitting the doctoral program remained. I still felt as if I left my old master behind, thus being punished with guilt. It would not go away until I embarked on a new journey, a 'real' journey. Lost, still. The circuits in my brain were firing at one another indiscriminatingly leaving me but a foggy path ahead. I could not see beyond a few yards. I could not think clearly about a specific thing I wanted to do, let alone which direction to take, no matter how hard I tried. Muddled thoughts made me more frustrated.

13. CLEAN

PROSCIUTTO, BRUSCHETTA, PHỞ, ARUGULA, COQ au vin, capers, caprese salad, steamed snapper, *bánh xèo*… had became my everyday challenges. Playing the role of a supportive wife of a composer was demanding. The musical academic world was completely different than any I had known before. I needed to attend concerts, receptions, and parties quite often with my husband. He and I also hosted receptions and dinners on a regular basis. When in a good mood, we planned a six-course menu. At the end of a semester with our energy drained, we settled on number three. Other times, we created a whole detail-oriented time-consuming Vietnamese cuisine menu. As our lives merged into one, these events turned into a matter of social survival for me. I put my best face forward and helped him plan, shop, cook, and present them with an efficiency I always knew I had in me but had forgotten existed. By doing so, I had tapped into myself to make something happen. Suddenly, it felt a little bit like an adventure—something I did not feel for a long while. At the same time, throughout all these occasions, I came to appreciate greatly the value of good social skills and creativity—the same crucial elements in the American practicality I liked so much and that I considered my favorite part in the American life. Seeing myself putting them at work revived in me the passion for exploration.

As this was happening, the foggy part in my brain started to melt away. I began to find some voice of my own as a self-aware naturalized citizen. The chase for degrees in an academic passage used to be my whole world, my only world, actually—a big sun right in front of my face as it was—now shrinking, diminishing. Slowly, from the periphery of my eyes, some new colorful rays emerged and caught my sight. The world far from the sun was huge out there and I was free to occupy any part of it. Some confidence dripped on me.

For the second time in the U.S., I realized I could do whatever I wanted as long as I was committed to it. The key was to know what I truly desired.

It was Fall again. The heat recedes and cooler weather draws people out into busy musical activities hiving around Bloomington like hard-working flapping bees. I arrived at a reception after a contemporary music concert and met a blond woman, A. She looked much older than the regular graduate students with whom I was familiar. Her voice, as she started to talk, was soft and high. Very excitedly, A. talked about the wonder of the human heart whose job is to pump blood in our body into 100,000 miles of vessels. "That is four times the earth circumference, can you believe that?" Her eyes sparkling.

I learned that she studied public health and that she would participate in an internship in Thailand next year. The word Thailand turned me on and the hook of the internship went deep beyond any interest I had in the field and pulled me along. Always being drawn to the idea of an internship abroad as another piece of American dream—a legitimate program that opens a window to the world giving one firsthand experience in exotic lands, I knew right then that I had to go to Thailand in the same program with A.

Well, Thailand is not necessarily exotic to me but in the current circumstances, any foreign land outside Bloomington sounded so alluring. I convinced myself a degree in public health would raise my chance of securing a better, more long-term job in Bloomington at a time when Obama healthcare gave people hope of universal health and the healthcare sector seemed to be growing and looking prosperous. I applied to the master's degree program in Public Health at IU and got in.

Working with books again, the old habit of hiding in the world of words re-emerged. I harbored the idea of a PhD degree in public health. *Everybody would be happy about this, anyway. What to lose.* My parents were happy that I was back to school. They began to hope again of someday seeing my doctoral degree hanging side by side those of my two other siblings. I glided through the classes, transfixing my hungry eyes on the dessert of the program, a two-month internship in Thailand.

In the summer of 2010, I got my work visa and went to Thailand.

There were two of us from Indiana University, A. and I, participating in the internship at Thaihealth. As a powerful non-profit organization, backed by the Thai government, Thaihealth conducted widespread and very effective anti-smoking campaigns all over Thailand. We were warmly received there. Thai colleagues treated us so kindly to lunch here and dinner there. They organized field trips for us and included us in their exchange activities with other international institutions. Their incredible friendliness and generosity were a real cultural treat for me.

That apart, it was both a matter of initiative and convenience of familiarity that I ended up leading the way in Thailand for the two of us. People outside Thaihealth, on the street, would not stop staring at A. and kept speaking Thai to me, probably because I looked Asian, as if I would translate back to A. what they said. I held no such linguistic advantage. In terms of real verbal communication, Caucasian A. and Asian me had only English to rely on. A. used more sign language to supplement. I listened more carefully and used very selective English words to deliver my message.

After the first few encounters, it occurred to me that in many ways the sight of me side by side with A. presented an unpalatable combination to Thai people. It reminded them of an imported tasteless bottle of wine, but a foreign product nonetheless with its own attraction. The stark differences between us made them want to dilute the flavors and smudge the colors of the wine to reach an unarticulated and desirable balance in it. It all reminded me of colonialism and how the power structure in the world worked. Thailand was not historically under colonialism. Their early encounters and dealings with Western forces plus the ominous impact of imperialism and globalization left marks of Western vestiges all the same.

Thai people smile a lot. Looking at tall, blond A. their smile broadened even more. It was fascinating to see how many of them were unable to resist the captivation of the 'white and blonde' trademark. Their pupils dilated and their jaws dropped, they swallowed every single word coming from A.'s mouth. As if hypnotized, they seemed to automatically render complete respect to the white person next to me. Turning to yellow-skin-dark-hair me they kept speaking Thai seemingly begging an interpretation to A. I appeared almost invisible in their eyes. It was devastating for me to experience this again, in a country I considered sisterhood and that bears cheerful, friendly and happy people. Our cultural or ethnic similarity does not stop at appearances. In our encounters with the West we strung our historical line dry with self-destructive hollows of fire. The seed of inferiority, intimidation and fear the imperialists planted in the minds of their subjects and the others had taken deep root and became a reflex in most of them. At the sight of a Western iconography, these people bow down.

I thought about Thai people's reactions a lot, the whole time I was in Thailand. It became an all-consuming affair about social behavior and representation. Just this glimpse to the surface of life in Thailand was enough for me to be heart-broken again seeing colonialism and imperialism at work beyond their masters' imagination hundreds of years later.

I was furious again. More than anything I was sad. I knew in Vietnam, the situation would be the same, even worse because of Vietnam's history of colonialism. I felt sorry for those Thai and Vietnamese who look up to Westerners just because their skin is white. For them to put me down in favor of white-skinned people the way they were brainwashed to believe that the whites were more superior in every way means that they look down on themselves. They may not be aware of it but they have used whatever power they have left in them, if any, to make themselves invisible in white people' s eyes. I hoped they recognized how outrageous and ironic that was and how much damage it did to their self-esteem.

To be fair, there were Thais who didn't care a hoot about who A. and I were and where we came from. They were busy enough with their own lives. And then there were these young, strong-minded, and intelligent women with who I made good friends. In spite of the language barrier, we got along very well. Because of them I began to think: Is it just me being so sensitive about the world around me? If I did not see and feel so much, my life would be easier.

At the end of the day, I knew my experience was real. More important, that I did not have a career in public health. It would be a wrong choice and a waste of time again to follow this path. Clear ideas began to form in my mind. *What I like to do is to write about my experiences, about how hilarious and ridiculous human life could become in this whole cultural mess we create for ourselves. The disturbing observations I had would continue to haunt me until I took action to deal with them properly.* For a second, I recognized that I had a strong voice and I needed to use it. No Vietnam War, no GIs and prostitutes. No refugees. No boat people. Those were not my stories to write. They were not the tales of my time.

While waiting for my thoughts to solidify into concrete plans of action, I tried to make the most out of the internship which turned out to be an exotic journey after all. Unable to make myself understood to Thai people, I could not help but plunge into the excitement of exploration. Getting lost in a cab and misunderstanding became memorable experiences to laugh at with friends. I felt the insatiable thrill in all of this as a blissful adventure to realize my dream. I introduced A. to the tropical fruits that I already knew such as longan, dragon fruit, durian, mangosteen, rambutan. I tried two new kinds of fruit we did not have in Vietnam, salak and kathon or santol. I tried almost all the new things I saw here, except fried bugs and crickets. I planned the out-of-town and around-town trips for the weekend. Sometimes I went with A. Sometimes by myself. I found great pleasure and satisfaction in orchestrating the solo trip to Ayutthaya, in standing under the heat of noon with the sun right above my head, to stare with awe at the thirteen century ruins, in utmost quietness having only my thoughts to listen to.

The two-month internship in Thailand was a highlight of my student career in America. My dream of an international internship was fulfilled. At the same time I could not deny that the thought about the PhD degree in public health happened on a whim—I would not want to be bitten twice. At least, I revisited my dream to make sure I was ready to drop it for good. I wasted my time, again, but the very action of doing something to try to get somewhere in life restored my confidence. I revived in myself the determination, the passion and the excitement of exploration.

At this moment of clarity and self awareness I realized what I had been doing in America all along was to act out both my suppressed and non-suppressed childhood desires. Via two master's programs and one doctoral program, I collected an MA degree in American Studies, another MA in American History, and an MS in Health Promotion. Like a child, I had been receiving all along, from people around me, friends and relatives in the U.S., new friends and mentors, and from life, to mold the world into my view.

I had been testing out my theory of American equality and democracy. According to that theory, in America, I could speak my mind and be considered equal to any. With satisfaction, I learned that many things I read in books about the American dream were true. That America is not a perfect country, but still a most special one where one's dreams could be fulfilled, at a steep price, of course.

Closing the door to the PhD degree, I could smile again. I eased up on taking fault for quitting the PhD program in history. I asked my parents to stop talking about the degree. It took them a few months to realize that I meant it. Then my father did stop talking about a PhD degree. Ironically enough, what actually convinced them, my father in particular, better than my spoken words were my written words. That was Fall of 2011.

I had tried to write something non-academic after the Thailand trip but every time I sat down at the computer, emptiness resounded. For a year I searched for ways to enter the first page. In the Summer of 2011, my husband and I were in Dresden, Germany. In this place where we least expected to see any Vietnamese, we found a fine Vietnamese restaurant owned by an artistic Vietnamese from Hà Nội. The restaurant occupied a highly visible spot in the center of the busiest restaurant quarter in old town Dresden.

Leaving the statue of Martin Luther at the Church of Our Lady behind and heading towards the Elbe river, we found ourselves enveloped in a lovely alley called Münzgasse. Lining up on both sides of it were a plethora of restaurants and bars of all tastes. In front of us was the beautiful Brühl's Terrace, a historic architectural ensemble nicknamed "The Balcony of Europe." The terrace stretches high above the shore of the river Elbe and serves as a perfect walking path embellished with more restaurants and coffee shops where tourists rest and enjoy the view of the river, the Augustus bridge on the left, and North Dresden beyond the river.

Halfway up the second flight of stairs to the terrace, we ran into the Vietnamese restaurant on our left. Surprised to see some Asian faces working the tables in there, we came in for a meal and a chat. That turned into a heart-warming conversation with a couple of Vietnamese students who worked there and went to Dresden University of Technology. It was completely stimulating to listen to them. Among two boys and a girl, they spoke fluent German, Chinese, Italian, and of course Vietnamese, and a little bit of Japanese. They were happy, confident, and excited about their future plans, whether those involved living abroad or coming back home to Hà Nội. Their presence was vibrant. Their enthusiasm contagious. Their energy palpable. They made me see that the past Vietnam I knew had become so outdated.

I was shocked. And fragments of lucidity fired up from the burner of my brain. I had lived in the U.S. for ten years, thinking I was in the best place to be in touch with time. What happened to me during that time had happened to many Vietnamese Americans before me. I met them ten years ago and thought I was not like them. I became one of them unawares. Like them, I was lost in a mind trap more powerful than the universe magnet: I had frozen my past, sleep-walked through my present and was blind to the future. It's the multiple loops of illusion that, once I break out of one, I fall into another. Unless.

And I thought I knew better.

After Dresden, we took the train to Prague. The first day there we ran into a young Vietnamese couple who had a grocery stall in a prime location of the old town. The husband, Trung, was from a northern city in Vietnam and the wife, Thương, a southerner. Trung came from a well-off family who had run their own business for many years. Yet, he wanted to explore the bigger world around him and to establish his own footsteps. He immigrated to Czech and stayed with his brother who helped him set up his own business. Two years later, confident and stable enough by himself, Trung moved out and started operating independently. His business was doing great. He usually took more than a month off in winter to travel. On one of those trips back home to Vietnam to visit his family, Trung met Thương and they fell in love. After getting married, Thương moved to Prague with Trung. Learning Czech and helping to run the grocery stall, Thương was devoted to building their business together. By the time we met her, Thương had lived in Prague about one year. She said the sadness of being away from home was over. She now looked forward to the future.

The amazing story of their efforts to carve out a new path in life for themselves in a new land moved me deeply. The encounters in Dresden and Prague were like serendipity playing tricks on my mind. In a matter of a few days, down poured a gnawing sense that the past was so ancient, the present so dead, and I did not have a lot of time to waste anymore.

I had done things in my life all wrong. I should have read books to step out of them, not to be buried in them. Better yet, a moment of real enlightenment happened when I recognized that there was no middleman between me and life—*I DID NOT HAVE TO GO THROUGH THE OLD AND THE DEAD TO GET TO LIFE*. That studying the way I did was not equivalent to action—it actually made me very passive. That is why, even after I got myself to the U.S., I still felt like a frozen statue on a page compared to people who were actually living life around me and who I often admired as my everyday heroes.

It was a subtle mental switch carriage that took half a lifetime train to arrive. Right then a large part of me was no longer (traditional) Vietnamese. The written words stopped exerting any commanding power over me. Right then, I found my way to achieve "the sense of action" in real life: One, reading books was not as cool a thing as being the one who created books. Two, quoting from others was not cool enough, either; I should be the one with original ideas that others quote from. *I will be a writer for real! It's a crazy ambitious plan. But what the heck, at 39 I still have more than twenty-five years ahead, meaning more than a quarter of a century, until retirement to make it work!*

Finally, I succeeded in breaking away from an old familiar academic tradition and dream. In a matter of seconds, the old me was erased from my consciousness. I started to celebrate the new one. The new me had only one important thing to do: create.

Back in Bloomington, I sat down and wrote Trung and Thương's stories and about the Vietnamese in modern times who disseminate all over the globe. Words splattered out from the laptop keyboard like water in a fall. Through the water veil I found a new door to enter the stories of my time.

Every morning I cannot wait to get up to write. One page a day. One hour a day. That is my daily dose of ecstasy that makes me high as a kite. Who needs Limoncello when writing ecstasy is free and guaranteed with no side effects. I write in Vietnamese and contribute to one of the three largest Vietnamese-language newspapers in the U.S. operating in Orange County of California. Shortly after I began writing, my father told me that he could see me doing this in the long run. And never mentioned a PhD degree anymore.

* * *

2000s—I have enjoyed our garden tremendously for years. I prune plants and cut flowers, bundle branches and saw trees. But weeding is my husband's job. I admire him for bending down to pull weeds with his bare hands without a single word of complaint. "It is relaxing," he says. I weed once in a while, always with a grimace on my face not really feeling any relaxation except the back pain.

2012—The wind was still this morning. We have had drought for almost a month. Hardly were we out to the yard because it was so hot. Weeds grew high to my knees. I stood and looked at them for a long moment, sighing. Then I opened the door, went outside, kneeled down and started pulling. The more I pulled the more I loved pulling more. Young weeds and old weeds were snatched off the ground with their long roots intact. To get a big chunk, I pressed my knees hard against the soil to keep balance, leaned forward and pulled with all my strength. My elbow made an upward jolt. With each movement of the elbow, I created a swift current that cracks the hot thick air. Then, not knowing where it came, I felt the lightness on my chest—spreading—as if some burden was lifted. Before I knew it, my heart was full of joy and an immense sensation of accomplishment. One bundle after another, I kept pulling until the area was clear of weeds. Clean.

My mind was serene. I typed these words using the same hands that I used to pull weeds—*and I am glad to use my hands for both.*

155

14. GIRL

As a young girl, I had a wild dream about marriage—a fancy, I would say, of getting hooked up with a white guy, specifically an American. Considering French colonization and American invasion in Vietnam, it may not be very strange. But it is not necessarily standard.

My mom, for example, had a certain distaste for American soldiers or cultural officers she saw in downtown Sài Gòn in the 1960s. Her friends or others talked to them but she kept a distance out of national pride. Maybe she talked to one or two at some point, but did not develop any special interest about those white-skinned blond-haired blue-eyed men and had no desire to get to know them better. Until much later in life when she came across the world of literary Nobel laureates and started translating their works into Vietnamese did she develop real interest in American culture and language.

My aunt Hương is a hardcore communist who does not believe in the seduction of America. She has a point, though. Her husband was killed in a South Vietnamese prison during the war, allegedly by poison.

So definitely, my partner preference did not come from the women I know well in my life. It was even a little strange given the exposure I had when small.

Living in an extended family, I could not help picking up things from seemingly insignificant events and carrying them with me like a kangaroo does a pouch—a second nature to have hidden yet not-so-hidden luggage with me—a visible yet not-so-noticeable characteristic that only comes in handy at fight-or-flight moments.

My grandfather was head of a family branch. Thus it was his responsibility to host all the important events and many guests. Death anniversaries were big and memorable events in a kid's life. During these occasions, my relatives from all over the country would visit. Some stayed with us for weeks, and attended the ceremony.

With guests around the kids had more leeway with usual nap time, homework, and bed time. Food was available all day long. And stories were exuding from every crack of the wooden floor for days on end. I would hang around to catch any droplets of them, from the living-room to the kitchen. The kids' favorite time was at night. The feast was over, people were now chatting over hot tea and coffee. The night began to get deep. Undistracted by the business of food and eating, these aunts, uncles, and grand-aunts and grand-uncles began to settle into a different rhythm. They lowered their voices and poured their hearts out. Stories about the dead and the living intermingled like currents of water spewing at the mouth of an estuary. All the scary yet irresistible ghost stories. Then there were so many other stories about so many people whirling in the air, people I knew and didn't know. It was overwhelming.

Four stories struck me the most. Two were about some great-grandfathers and the other two some fiery aunties. Every year some tales about them would be told and retold. They all sounded so fascinating every single time, if not more so. They were like a snow-ball rolling down a hill in a storm that gets bigger and bigger with things it picked up along the way (to borrow an image my former mentor D.H. told me once).

One great-great-grandfather was a court mandarin. He did not hold a doctorate degree like many of his peers but was so talented and wise he was granted the court title of Ngự Sử, or Advisor to the King. This title made him a mandarin of the highest rank in the realm. This was obviously a huge honor to himself and the big family. At the gathering everybody still clicked their tongues and talked about him with pride. I thought he was really cool.

Another great-grandfather, my dad's grandfather, was also a court mandarin with a voice very deep and loud. The relatives around the table said that everybody in the household would hear him calling from the front house. He was as kind to the grand kids as he was big and tall. Proportionally, his built matched so well with his personality at moments he confronted, yelled at, and even whacked some French officers. He did these things quite often. Everybody in the family, as well as those working with and for him, and people around him admired him for the fact that he had absolutely no respect, let alone fear, for the whites. I thought *this* was so brave and extremely thrilling. The fact that he was really big and tall in real life, at six feet, seemed almost enough to win my tiny heart at seven or eight. When I grew a bit older I began to notice that he had more than one wife. I was not fond of this fact but still very much impressed by his personality. He remained my man.

"And auntie Ái here as we all know," uncle Cẩm would then chime in, his voice ringing like a brass bell, "she is a true Hoàng woman in her own manner. Even the high-ranking Party leaders showed her respect." Auntie Ái joined the revolutionary force at the age of sixteen in the 1920s to fight French colonialism and continued on to become a communist. Very sharp and courageous, she held different positions in the party over time and was still very active as an octogenarian.

And there is auntie Hoằng. At 70, her white hair was long and shining. She often braided it in the back and tied up the sides very artfully. Her skin glowed and blushed like that of a baby's making other women so envious. She was another fiery fighter during the war. After the Geneva Treaty in 1954, when Vietnam was temporarily divided into two waiting for the general election to be scheduled, she moved north with her husband to continue fighting for the liberation forces. Around the dining table, she talked about surviving in the jungles—the heat and the rain and all the diseases.

She survived the weeks-long bombings in 1972 in Hà Nội. As uncle Cẩm, uncle Tú and others finished telling the story, auntie Hoằng commented here and there to confirm the facts. Many of the male adults would then end their stories with a familiar remark: "A true Hoàng woman, indeed."

I know that the Hoàng family is well-known in the original hometown of Bích Khê village in Quảng Trị because there were many high-ranking mandarins in the genealogy. I did not know what they meant by "a true Hoàng woman, indeed." They only talked like that about the women within the family. Aunties did not seem to be very ferocious to me. I sneered at their comment and thought of it as the clumsy effort of men who were not so comfortable at complimenting women in public but who were now pouring their hearts out after a few glasses of rice wine. Yet, I admired those Hoàng women and felt proud about them. They did not like the white guys, either.

Then there is my father who is an aficionado of the English language. He often joked with his friends that he must have been an Englishman in his previous life! He adores the English language and British and American literature, as well as American actors and actresses such as Gregory Peck, Audrey Hepburn, Marlon Brando, James Dean, Humphrey Bogart, Marilyn Monroe, Elizabeth Taylor, etc. And also Alain Delon, Catherine Deneuve, Brigitte Bardot, etc.

He had a treasure.

I remember the first time I touched something close to a real evidence of the American presence in Vietnam—it was the pages from the *Life* magazine. My dad had tons of them, literally about a ton in weight of them, stacked in the attic. Right after the war ended in 1975, that kind of material was not something people would keep around for fear of stigmatization of the old regime. Around and after the fall of Sài Gòn, the city people took anything they considered a remnant of South Vietnam and burned them all. My dad kept all the English books and magazines. You could be put in jail for possessing such materials, I heard. I had no idea how he did not get into trouble. His love affair with the language must have made it impossible for him to part with them. By the time I found them, they were old and yellow. The issues on top and bottom suffered the most from rainwater leaking from the roof or splattering from the windows. The stains smeared the words. They were unintelligible and the images unrecognizable. My dad would not need to see those words anyway as he must have been done studying them. As for me, forget about the words, it was the pictures that drew me in.

I untied the strings, put the damaged issues away, and started turning the intact pages. Staying stiff in the bundle for so long they made crackling sounds. Among the dust caking around the edges, I found a lot of words, but even more pictures, some of them as large as the double page itself. I felt overwhelmed at the saturation of colors and close-up details. Many times I had to stretch my little arms the furthest I could to keep the pages afar and have a good look at the pictures. When that was not good enough, I laid the pages on the floor and stood up looking down at them. The cranes were flying off to the pink-orange sky. I heard their calls echo in the still air as their long legs were just leaving the dark green grass field. Then a lot of green trees in a forest. A winter forest white with snow. Lots of pictures of the actors and actresses. I especially liked the picture of a couple. A well-suited man with short clean-cut smooth hair. He looked sharp. And a beautifully dressed woman. I liked her dress, simple and elegant. Her bob hair was neat; she was smiling and looked happy. They were standing by a red car parked in front of a lake. The morning white light was shining from above and its shimmering reflection on the water glittering in front of my eyes. "Happy! Happy!" was the silent exclamation I felt looking at them.

I tore off the pictures of the cranes, Hollywood actors, and the happy couple, folded them and took them to my room. Fearing that my dad would reprimand me for tearing off the pages from his treasure, I pressed them carefully in one of my books and put it in the furthest corner of the shelf among the old-looking books. I was about ten or eleven. I recalled this moment to be the earliest one when I must have had the faintest perception about romance and success, about how I perceived the happy man and woman to ideally look like in a relationship. I had been carrying this image all along unawares.

* * *

I must have been born a mute child of a philosopher. In junior high, I could watch the boys' games to impress the girls without any reaction. I thought they were all childish. Then my rebellious years rolled in and stretched to college, with more disappointing boys' games and more silent observations.

In tenth grade, I read Kim Định because I wanted to find out what my name meant. Kim Định was a Vietnamese Catholic priest-philosopher-researcher-scholar-professor-writer with whom my mom studied at the University of Sài Gòn in the 60s. She had more than ten of his books in the house. She loved his theory so much she named me after it, An-Vi. An-Vi is the term coined by Kim Định to refer to what he called "philosophy of the Vietnamese." He spent ten years in France studying and researching Eastern and Western philosophy, civilization, and archeology before coming back home to teach and write his book series. These books about Vietnamese culture and philosophy mesmerized me. Because of Kim Định, I knew then that I wanted to spend the rest of my life doing something about Vietnamese culture.

One year before going to college and throughout college years, while the *Life* pages were tucked in an old book on the shelf, I tapped into a world full of real English words, some at school but the most interesting of these I stumbled upon the same way I did the *Life* pages.

I had been eyeing my dad's books all those years but could not read any because they were in English—until now. When my father was not home I took a few to my room. I thought, with so many books around, he would not possibly know what was missing. I also did not want him to know what I read.

A few weeks later he came to my room and asked whether I had borrowed some of his books. So much for him not noticing. Yet the childish thievery was rewarding.

Apart from Emily Brontë's *Wuthering Heights* and George Bernard Shaw's *Pygmalion* as two real books I was assigned to read in college, a few poems and short stories here and there were all we learned. On my dad's shelves, on the other hand, I found Oscar Wilde's *The Importance of Being Earnest*, William Faulkner's *The Sound and the Fury*, Khalil Gibran's *The Prophet*. I also came across Freud, Schopenhauer, Kant, Kierkegaard, Jaspers, Hemingway, Saul Bellow, Emerson, Hawthorne, Twain, and many others. And, of course, Shakespeare. While Marxism was the official theory taught at school, my finds were like pirate treasures that turned up on a beach after the violent night tides. They presented a wondrous world to me. I gobbled *The Sound and the Fury* and *The Prophet* cover to cover, wrote a paper on *The Importance of Being Earnest*, and kept the rest around so I could turn their pages for a passage here or a line there, whenever I was bored, stuck with something on my mind, or lost in meandering thoughts. What I eventually learned from these books was that I was very sure about life and how I handled my life.

One year before going to college, I also started listening to and recording the BBC programs religiously. There were English teaching programs, news, theater, hit songs, story reading, sports, interviews of all sorts, etc. I listened to them, recorded them, listened to them again, took notes, transcribed them, listened to them again and again to complete my notes and transcriptions, then labeled all the tapes carefully and stacked them in boxes. Year in year out, the boxes of tapes were growing out of control. Amidst these sometimes crystal clear recorded words and sometimes muffled radio words, Queen's English became the favorite melody of my ears. I mimicked it the best I could.

Mysterious and fascinating as the way many things in life work, in spite of my utmost adoration for British English to the last enunciation, clarity came to me in the form of the printed words.

The day I picked up *The Prophet* I felt high for months. I lived in Khalil Gibran's English words. My usual sensibility was disrupted. From his writing, I soaked up the deepest sense of equality and freedom that a human soul could possibly experience. From that moment on, in my mind, whatever I wanted and had been searching for in the world out there, it was in America. In this bizarre concoction of thoughts, desires, beliefs and emotions, America was out there for me. That was where I would find what I was looking for. And whatever I wanted to do I knew it would have to include both cultures.

For six years after graduation I taught English as a Second Language. A lot more thinking and searching happened. People may say we cannot operate in a vacuum but I disagree. In Vietnam, we operated, and still do, in a vacuum all the time. I grew up with socialism and communism. What I remember most is the gender equality agenda. We were taught that men and women were equal. *I never thought otherwise, anyway.* During that time, the non-discriminatory nature of life quality and relationships among us in post-war hardships could have been working in tandem with the prolonged innocence of Vietnamese children. In peace and shortages we really took time to grow up. The years of diplomatic isolation from the world around us turned our world into something as mysterious as a black hole. The mixture of Marxism, Leninism, bits of Russian language and literature, crumbs of Chinese literature, a few British and American stories and poems, even a tad of Australian culture, all fell through the hole leaving it as empty as ever. My generation grew up in a vacuum. It was where we preserved our innocence, and probably a lot of ignorance about the world around us.

I was lucky to be able to sprinkle my adolescence and adulthood with some Western-American confetti preserving for myself a very colorful innocence and idealism. From this viewpoint, I consider my experience with Vietnamese male friends to be as idealistic as my encounter with American culture was problematically idiosyncratic. Fragmented. Both idealism and fragmentation were good things because they collided to create a crack through which I got myself out of the hole.

Very often, facing me on the other side of the table, a man. We were in a café. The lights dimmed to the right ambience and instrumental music played softly in the background. I sat on the cushioned velvet booth chair with mirrors all around. Once accustomed to the light and shadow of the place, I was able to see the reflective expressions on his face. He had been my good friend for many years; he was kind and all that. I would ask him: "Why do you look at me and see a girl, while I look at you and see a human being?"—this particular question in English and not Vietnamese. He smiled and said nothing. There's nothing funny about the question. I felt rage welling up in me. I did not think he understood what I tried to say but his body language told me that he saw through me. In his thoughts, he saw me as a sweet innocent girl, and he was in a higher place with no intention to come down.

I was very familiar with the world of thoughts. My ancestors were stuck in it unable to move forward. They were so focused on the endeavor to strive for some meaning in life, to achieve beauty and sophistication in motionless reality. Thoughts and written words were their world. These thoughts and words did not challenge them, neither reject them; gave them meaning, security, and a sense of satisfaction—in a way, perfect satisfaction in the pursuit of delusional perfection. To them, spoken words were not efficient and powerful enough to express their feelings so intense, pure, and elevated. Therefore, thoughts in the mind would do the job for them. Their whole world was dominated by just thoughts. Thoughts-and-thoughts-and-thoughts swallowed whole their life. They became numbed, unable to act.

Thoughts used to be my main diet. But I was also always looking for actions.

Thus, as I was coming of age and beyond, I became very disappointed by the passivity and immaturity of boys-men around me. Stories like that of great-grandfather, *my man*, who yelled at the

French officer, gradually became a myth to be replaced by a reality that I heard about more often and believed in more and more. Relatives and acquaintances who married Americans, Australians or Frenchmen often said that foreign men were nicer, more gallant, and more open-minded than Vietnamese men.

When I turned 25, more and more friends and relatives pressured me on the issue of marriage. Luckily, my parents did not. We would not have listened to them, anyway. So, "You'll be a spinster being so picky, I warn you!" my good friend would say. "How much longer do you want to wait for Mr. Right? He may not exist, you know," said another. The unsolicited advice from them was to compromise. "You cannot have everything. There must be something you are willing to sacrifice," they said. I was determined to find the right person.

Looking around, the lack of equality and freedom for women and progress stifled me. Every time there was a gathering, be it an anniversary or a social function, all the women would gather in the kitchen sweating over the food and drink. In the living-room, the men were crossing their legs in the couch enjoying tea, talking politics (as if they know real politics). I loathed the scenes.

In the modern era, my country has experienced more than a hundred years juggling ideas of liberty, freedom, and democracy. Then a few more dozen years trying to digest socialism and communism. All these many years combined were nothing compared to centuries grappling under the yoke of feudalism and Confucianism. Before me now, the outdated Confucius traditions were choking life out of its women victims. Gasping for fresh air to breathe became an urgent demand to me.

Everyday life was messy and miserable. Most local government officials made it their job to 'harass' the citizens as much as they could for bribes, or for the heck of it, instead of helping them to get things done. It was unfortunate if I needed a stamp from a ward officer on a document. Having heard so many stories about bribes and mishaps in cases of confrontation, I would walk to their office being so nervous and scared. An encounter with a non-smiling, sometimes very cranky, government official was like an interrogation. It could become a wild goose chase that no one could predict when and where it would end, as I was sent from one office to another for a 'right' red stamp. In spite of it and because of it, people were so afraid to raise any questions or to take any kind of action against it. *Something bad could happen to me*, they calculated; and the sentiment spread. This culture of fear was very corrosive towards self-esteem and self-confidence. It did not show signs of stopping anytime soon.

By this time, I also grew so sick of the prolonged ignorance I had to endure throughout my life. I was teaching in a system where most people in charge did not know what they were doing simply because they were not qualified to hold any position. Bachelor-degree holders teaching to-be bachelor's degree graduates was not a valid method of doing things. Personally, I did not consider it ideal that I was teaching a college class, me being equipped with only a bachelor's degree—even when my command of English was excellent. I wanted higher education for myself so I could do an outstanding job as a professor. I wanted better education for millions of Vietnamese around me.

There were graduate programs available in a few fields. Most of them were a sham then. The research environment was non-existent. Textbooks were full of errors. I could not trust published materials out there. The quality of education was going downhill daily leaving it to individuals to fend for themselves. Right under my nose, the popular culture of fear and ignorance made up the hallmarks of Vietnamese life under communism. I was terrified of ignorance more than anything else. It was like living in an enclosed dark cave waiting for the oxygen to run out. The thought that I might die before having a chance to see the world and getting rid of my number one enemy—ignorance—terrified me. *I could not take it any longer*, I told myself.

Since the early 1990s Vietnamese overseas began to come back to visit their families and their country in large numbers. Vietnamese people at home began to talk a lot about 'democracy.'

With pervasive ignorance around, the only thing that 'their democracy' led to was hypocrisy and an inflated sense of action. There was nothing democratic in it when the people who talked about it still held deep-set feudalistic behavior and believed that they were above others. They believed sitting around criticizing everything and everyone for fun was already 'progressive' enough. In my book, 'democracy' must be 'better' than that. Confident that they did not know what they were talking about, I disregarded those pseudo activists. Any bits of information about 'democracy' floating out there were misinterpreted, or incomplete at best. I had to get out of all this mess before it took over me and turned me into a bitter person like many around me. *I had to experience democracy firsthand.*

These days I have learned to recognize the multi-headed Medusa of 'democracy' but back then, idealism was all I had. Because of it, the belief I had in the power of the word 'America' grew stronger everyday.

Tết was around the corner. My mom and the four of us set our hearts on the annual ritual cleaning spree. We cleansed and painted the house upside down and inside out. Then I reorganized my bookshelf. I took the books off, dusted them, and reviewed them for discard. As more dust was released into the air, I found the old *Life* pages in a book. I unfolded them and looked at the beautiful cranes and the forest. I remembered keeping them because they were pleasant to the eye. But why the Hollywood movie stars?! I threw them away. There was also the picture of a handsome couple advertising for a car. Somewhat puzzled at the finding—"Why did I keep this ad?" I thought aloud.

I threw them all away. There was no point in keeping these pages while America was just across the ocean.

I started planning.

* * *

In the early 1990s a computer meant a golden goose. Normal folks like us had to come to a computer house and pay to use one. Some people with money would equip one room in their house with a dozen computers and rent them out by the hour. People with more money would use one or two rooms downstairs and one or two rooms upstairs in their house for computer rentals. It was good business.

Before the decade came to an end, not only the computer but also the internet became more affordable for home use in Vietnam. I had a good job then and was more than capable of chipping in with my brothers and sister to buy a computer and pay for the internet service. Playing with the chunky monitor, the floppy disks, and the internet, in 1998 I began searching for a scholarship to America.

I believed strongly in the fairness of the system, that anything could happen in America. I emailed different universities and asked for the applications. The U.S., under the Clinton administration, only normalized diplomatic relations with Vietnam in 1995. Information began to flow in. I did not know a single thing about universities in America. But I found St. Andrews University in North Carolina, if I remember correctly.

The day the first brochure arrived was pretty magical, as if I had found a direct line to enlightenment. Holding the brochure, I thought: "I really like the way American people work!" In total I received three of them including the University of Denver in Colorado, I think, and one more I don't remember anymore. I was searching for a program in American Studies but found nothing. Determined to succeed, I continued my search in the precious copies of the *Economist, Newsweek* and *Times* magazines. I looked for university names. Now, these magazines were not yet readily available on the stands at the time, or were exorbitantly expensive. It happened that my father had a student who was an airline attendant. He had access to such kinds of magazines. He would often collect and save the old editions for my dad. That was how my father came to possess stacks of them and how I had access to them as well.

Before I found anything else, BYU happened.

At the time of normalization and after, a hot topic in Vietnam was globalization. It was all about cultural understanding and people around the world holding hands singing kumbaya. Everywhere, people played *We Are The World* with Michael Jackson as one of the soloists, and the magnanimous "Imagine" by John Lennon. Before Christmas, during and after Christmas. Then New Year. Before, during and after Tết. Women's Day. Children Day. Teachers' Day. Almost year round. *We are the world, we are the children. We are the ones who make a brighter day, so let's start giving. There's a choice we're making. We're saving our own lives. It's true we'll make a better day, just you and me. Imagine there's no countries. It isn't hard to do. Nothing to kill or die for. And no religion, too. Imagine all the people. Living life in peace. You may say I'm a dreamer. But I'm not the only one. I hope someday you'll join us. And the world will be as one.*

Bathing in this soothing sentiment, Vietnamese women understood feminism as a movement to advocate gender equality at home and in the workplace, and the free will of all human beings. The image of a strong-willed, independent woman who works to make her own living and her own choices—like a Western woman, is our—or my—role model. And most importantly we believed the movements spoke for and included yellow skin people like us over here in Vietnam. We felt a part of it.

Thus, Vietnamese culture and language, and American culture and language became my goals. I left the country with utmost confidence that I would find in America not only modernity, equality, democracy, and a way to promote Vietnamese culture, but also my Lancelot.

15. LIBERATED

ONCE IN AMERICA, I WAS ecstatic about the possibility of conversing with Americans on a daily basis. The very first one was Joyce, my housemate. Her talking sounded like singing because of the musical tone in her voice. The other first ones, I met on the bus.

One morning, I got on it and saw an old man already seated. It was summer and he was wearing a white suit. He also had a vest and tie on. I said "Good morning" to him smiling. (Yes, I had already learned to smile when greeting.) He also smiled and responded in kind. I settled down and looked toward him with curiosity. His long hair and beard were all white, even his eyebrows were white. In my Vietnamese thinking, he looked like a sage ready to disseminate words of wisdom. He returned my look, smiled and said to me: "You are incredibly beautiful." A little surprised, I responded "Thank you." And being puzzled by the comment, I stayed quiet after that.

At the time I was expecting a more interesting conversation with the sage-looking man. I was a little disappointed that it did not happen.

Also on some of these first encounters, people would ask me: "Where are you from?" "Vietnam," I said. I saw bafflement on their faces at the sound of 'Vietnam', as if they did not know where it was. Quite shocked, I told them Vietnam was in Southeast Asia and saw more puzzlement. I took one second to think. Then told them that Vietnam was a country right next to China. They went, "Oh!" The muscles on their faces relaxed and their eyes lit up.

Very soon I learned that the world knew so little about my country except the controversial Vietnam War, that I was very different from Americans, from the way I looked and talked to the way I behaved, and that people would see me as such. "It is the country next to China" became my standard response to "Where are you from?" Over time, I embellished it a little: "If you look at the map and see the S-shaped country (*yeah, like it helps!*) south of China, that is Vietnam." This whole detective-pleading episode elevated my pride not one nano-centimeter higher. Quite the opposite.

Year in year out, I was learning about the world. It was now the twenty-first century, and gender inequality was still a serious issue, especially in Asia and the Middle East. Even here in the U.S., women were paid less than men for the same kind of work. In China, baby girls were killed at infancy because their parents preferred sons. When the sons grew up and faced a reality of women shortage, kidnapping girls from neighboring countries such as Cambodia and Vietnam became the new practice. These women became the breeding brides for the Chinese families. I learned about these kidnaps during the time I was in America and became so furious. Homesickness only made the pain and the rage I felt more visceral. I was extremely frustrated about the fact that China was bullying its way in the world and getting away with it.

After 9/11 the U.S. became a country gripped by panic and fear. Then increased instability in Iraq as the American occupation there dragged on after the 2003 invasion signified to me that understanding between human beings, the hope for peace, and the return of the old world in the U.S. to where it was before the bombing were zero; that reasoning was overrated; that the world was operated on stereotypes and violence. Terms such as cultural understanding or multiculturalism used to mean a great deal to me; they now became so hollow; and being a minority in America was a tricky thing.

The depressing picture of the world made me feel as if what I was doing in the U.S. was trying to knock down a brick wall with my head and these attempts gave me vertigo. Then, as the world was spinning and stars popping up in front of my eyes, I caught sight of many great schemes stirring around so insidious and intriguing. I was sucked in and became a part of them—I enjoyed the game, too.

One afternoon, I was using the computer in the main library at IU when a man approached me. "You looked so familiar. I thought we had met before, hadn't we," he said. "I don't think so," I responded, not smiling. "Oh, you are so beautiful. With black hair and brown eyes, you look just like many of the Filipino friends I have. You don't happen to come from the Philippines, do you?" he asked me. I could not help a dry laugh. I said no. "Where are you from?" he insisted. *I could not believe this guy.* I turned on my game playing mood and told him to guess. "Korea?" "No." "Japan?" "No." "China?" "No." "Thailand?" "No." "Cambodia?" "No." "Then I give up," he said.

"Vietnam," I told him.

"I could never have guessed!" he exclaimed.

He was a middle-aged man. His well-fitted black suit did great justice to his slim built. His curly hair touched his shoulders and his black eyes appeared non-threatening. I knew he thought he was being charming and nice giving me compliments like that. Maybe he did not know that he was patronizing me. Maybe he did. But he probably did not know that I saw through him. There was no reason, but I felt sorry for the guy. More importantly, I was disappointed and angry at myself for not being able to use confrontation effectively to express myself.

What he did to me was a subtle form of discrimination: he carried out racial and cultural assumptions about me. Not being able to understand the delicate relations between countries in the region, he lumped me into the Asian pile. Historically, politically, and diplomatically, Cambodia, China, Korea, Japan, the Philippines, Thailand, and Vietnam shared an intricate map of friendship and power among themselves, within Asia and the rest of the world. To locate a cultural trace that every single one of them agrees to say they share in common was non-existent. I remember one of the first things I learned in America was to respect individualism, and to always keep in mind that people are different and they don't want to be compared to one another. It made sense even for me not to be overly eager to claim a shared Asian cultural trace with other Asians.

Here I was, being bundled like a bogo deal in a sale at Payless Shoe store. Being hurtful was an understatement. As a subtle form of racism and discrimination, cultural assumptions or biases are difficult to recognize and hard to deal with because there is barely hard evidence of them to collect. Nonetheless, they are illegal and punishable under the law. *Are they? They should be!* Frustration and depression are the least two imprints they leave behind.

And why was it so difficult for the man to understand this while Americans did the same thing trying to separate their identity from their predecessors? Among other things, they managed to prove that American English was distinguishable from British English. I once received a mass email that had been circulated around like a hot cake among English learners: the list of American and British vocabularies compiled with the sole aim of comparing and contrasting the particular ways in which people of the two nations have used their language. For example, a truck in America is a lorry in England; flavor is American English while flavour is British English; et cetera. That was only the linguistic aspect we talk about here!

There was no wind in the library, and yet, I seemed to see the good-looking man's hair flying violently in the air taking away with it the dead kumbaya song.

Never before could I imagine that one day my own world would become that spiced up. I did not plan any of those moments. They came rushing at me. Through those experiences, finding nuances in the tone of voice, the slight turn of the lips in the smile, or the dark sparkle in the eyes, I figured out the comfort or discomfort, sympathy or guilt, ignorance or recognition that American people experienced or displayed when facing me. There was no hiding from them because when it came to Vietnam, there was not much to work with. 'Vietnam' meant only a few things in the American national psyche: the Vietnam War, GIs and prostitutes, or refugees. I could easily detect what image they had in mind when the word

'Vietnam' rang in their ears. Nowadays the list includes *phở* and *bánh mì*.

The more I think about the experiences the more comical they become. The same feeling I had when the joke was on me in this cartoon I found a while ago and still remember.

It was a cover on the *Times* or the *Economist*. In the center was a tiny skinny guy bending his knees trying to balance the back-breaking weight put on him. He had both his hands above his head. On one palm, he was carrying a little fat guy called China, and on the other a big tall chubby one called the U.S. Both the China and the U.S. guys were shaking hands. Their other hand, however, they put in the back, their fingers crossed. The poor guy who was almost crushed by the weight he was carrying was named Vietnam.

The nationalistic part in me interpreted the cartoon as extremely disturbing because it described how imperialistic dealing was at work in the twenty-first century and how people still cheered on it. At the same time, the critical thinking part in me had to admit that the cartoon picture was hilarious and very clever. It captured perfectly the nature of the relations between the three countries. Many scholars could spend years writing books to analyze those relations and still might not get close to portraying a clear picture to the reader the way that cartoon did visually. Its clarity made it impossible for me to forget—it made me laugh and cry at the same time.

And the headache from the vertigo remained with me.

As more young men approached me, I still did not learn the art of confrontation because every time it took a different shade and shape. They never repeated. The only thing I gained was more frustration and rage. My mind became so saturated with the screaming episodes that I would run many times again and again in my head trying to find the best way out of them. They made me see more weight being put on the bony guy. At some point I transferred to become the skinny guy in the real cartoon of my life, struggling with the weight upon my shoulders. I did not bother to discern how American people saw me and I did not want to take a chance. I would probably get disappointed, I told myself. To protect myself, I began to armor up at my best. Like a robot, I pre-screened to reject people who approached me on the observation that I looked Asian. Using the same tricks they did, with the slightest alteration in my voice, body language, or my stare, I pushed them away. Not just guys, I shielded up on anyone who bordered on judging me based on some assumption about my culture.

The sad thing was that I behaved differently in so many ways than a typical American, which facilitated questions and curiosity about my ethnicity.

In the end, it was like a vicious cycle with no way out for me. The anger for being viewed as a girl rushed back. This time it was worse. Double-labeled, I was either an Asian girl or a Vietnamese girl.

The need to have to explain and defend myself and my culture all the time was physically debilitating and psychologically exhausting.

* * *

It is cold in Bloomington in the winter. On average there is only one big snowstorm a year and not so much snow here compared to Indianapolis and the northern parts of the state. Yet, that is cold enough to feel the chill in my bones as I get older. When I expressed the sentiment to a Swedish friend, he laughed, banged on the table and told me: "There is no such thing as cold weather, only bad clothing." And he laughed some more.

Later on, I went out and bought the warmest down coat available in the store. I did not like the fact that it was made in China, but I had no choice. America is overrun by products made in China. When the anti made-in-China-products sentiment rises, the manufacturers do their trick and change the label to Made in PRC. Not everyone knows that PRC is (People's Republic of) China. Putting the coat on, I looked at myself in the mirror. I understood why most Vietnamese want to settle in Orange County, California, or Houston, Texas. The coat almost swallowed me whole. It is near ridiculous to shift our tropical weather body across the Pacific Ocean and make it acclimated to the blizzard of the mid-west or the east coast. Nothing natural about it.

Not to mention I was lonely in Bloomington. Until I met my super-friend, the Vietnamese American composer-professor, P.Q. Phan. He has lived more than half of his life in the U.S., that's nearly a quarter of a century. The only professional Vietnamese American creative artist in his field, he constantly knocks down barriers, common assumptions, standard interpretations, misinterpreted statements, and walls around him to build his road path, alone. I learned a lot from him.

"Do you know that Vietnamese people in the U.S. try very hard to get rid of their accent in speaking English? At the same time, the Europeans do the opposite to preserve their European accent, because it is revered over here," he spurted out one day, just like that. "What this tells you about America is that, etc." I was often swept off my feet by observations like that one. I thought about it and it's true that Vietnamese people opt for adaptation, assimilation, trying to shave off their edges, while the Europeans guard their essence and differences.

Another time, also in our long conversations about history and cultural differences, it must have been the hidden adaptation sense he uncovered in my thinking that made him throw out this surprisingly terse comment: "You don't want an American guy. You want a person who could understand Vietnamese culture."

I was speechless.

He was very perceptive, direct and honest—and he seemed to shake me back to sanity. My armor was down, yet I felt very safe. I was used to his strong headedness before. He often held very original opinions deviating completely from the traditional Vietnamese thinking I grew up with. This moment now hit me that my friend's spoken words conveyed *actions*. A person with an opinion who is not afraid to express it meant a lot of *action* to me. Going through the traditional Vietnamese upbringing full of restraints and repression, I witnessed people around me quoting others to show off instead of making use of self-expression and creativity. I used to hide behind some names and quotes as well, like a nasty habit that infectiously clung to one's soul once taken root. I had trained myself to break away from those traditions. And I had been looking for people who knew how to take real *action*.

You don't want an *American guy*. You want a *person* who could understand Vietnamese culture. I sensed a strong fighting spirit in him. His statement made me see that, even though I did intentionally resist a white man's approach, I was uncontrollably pulled towards it in some degree. I called this haunting suction an ancestral sin, the most ancient and popular yet best kept secret of all. It registered automatic submission to Western power deep beyond my muscular control.

I know it because I inherited a sad history of Vietnam and the ancestral sin was in my kangaroo pouch. That is why all along what I had carried with me, in the subconscious part of my mind, was the physical image of a big tall guy who was white. In my kangaroo pouch there were also my great-grandfather's spirit and my grandmas' glowing free will. This recognition, like an antidote, saved me at every turn. Every time I was unwittingly geared towards the physics, my stubborn cognizance reminded me that so far I was not able to associate an *American guy* with equality, freedom and happiness. That I definitely left out the rest of the whole picture.

P.Q. continued to talk. Part of me was listening to him, another part busy processing the changes in my mind. As I shifted my focus from a white guy to a human being, I finally saw the paradox in which I was living. As if my friend was trying to fight in my place waiting for me to pick up my own fight to shed my fallacy, the second he made that statement, he unintentionally cleared up the clouds covering my great-grandfather's image. I saw my old man again standing big and tall waging his hands and whacking the French guys. I regained faith in the existence of people like him. Right before my eyes stood an Asian-looking guy who had travelled the world. He had the most fascinating stories about his parents and grandparents, about Vietnam, and about people all over the globe to tell me. He cooked like a chef. He absorbed so many cultures within himself he could challenge anybody and any idea.

He had crushed the last piece of illusion in me. It was time I admitted to myself the bare truth about my dream, to face the reality that my soul mate did not have to be a big tall white guy. I did not come to the U.S. to look for any kind of approval from anyone to be happy. Neither did I have any desire to be confined in my own expectations. My friend made me see that I had the power to free myself and make myself happy. The choice was in my hands.

Like a passer-by who woke up sleeping beauty with a bucket of cold water, he was more Vietnamese than anyone I had met before, yet he was more American than I could ever imagine.

Eighteen months later we got married.

* * *

After marriage, I decided to keep my last name. Even though I only followed the Vietnamese tradition just like American women do in changing their last name, I could not deny the descending flush of pride. I am sure, with the patriarchal system in existence for more than a thousand years, the Vietnamese tradition has nothing to do with, in fact it is anything but, a manifestation of equality or women liberation. But I chose to reinterpret this Vietnamese last-name-keeping tradition I practiced in the U.S. as an act of empowerment on my part.

Three years on, I was disappointed that the Vietnamese last name separate from that of my husband's did not bring me a sweep of prowess as strong and monumental as I wished it would to assist me in my course of life. It did nothing to protect me against inquisitions about my ethnicity. I looked around and compared myself to other Vietnamese Americans I know who married white men and changed their last names. Their lives seemed to be full of action. Their friends list on Facebook looked more diverse, and they sounded more assertive. As if a foreign last name added power to themselves. A Vietnamese first name and a foreign last name appeared so exotic. It blurred some borders and crossed some lines—and I liked that feeling. You even have to twist your tongue a little and enunciate a little harder to pronounce the whole name—and I liked the hard work.

It was just a passing thought. I felt ashamed to even have it in my head. It was disgusting, the lingering ancient sin of desire for foreignness. It felt like cheating. I caught myself red-handed just in time to banish the comparison and the desire for good.

By the time I got my citizenship, defense over my identity and culture took on a new layer of meaning. My everyday challenges were familiar yet new at the same time.

One day I came to the Social Security Administration office. A clerk behind the glass window offered to help me. I told them that they misallocated my gender in the file and they needed to fix that. Without a blink, the clerk started talking to me very slowly and loudly, almost like she was dictating. I knew too well that many Americans talked to international students this way to show their kindness and understanding, or patronization, about the fact that English was not our mother tongue. I appreciated it the first few times, but it had to stop at some point. They needed to stop assuming that I was an international student. Feeling disturbed, while she was talking to me I was screaming in my head: "I guarantee you that I could write English more correctly than you do and I could make a far more superior presentation than you could ever imagine!" I could not wait for her to finish her sentences.

When it was my turn to talk, I told her that her office made a mistake not the BMV office. That was why the BMV people sent me here. "You cannot possibly send me back there," I said. I spoke very fast. I did not know if she understood me clearly via the glass window but she started repeating herself telling me to go to the BMV, slowly and loudly. She drove me crazy. I suddenly thought maybe I needed to be louder. I increased my volume. She heard me this time. For a soft-spoken person I was, I sounded like shouting already. And I did not like that.

When I got out of the office, I started replaying the episode in my head. I was so mad at myself for giving the clerk a chance to patronize me. Again, she may not know that she was patronizing me with all her assumptions. A part of me wished I could have yapped at her slowly and loudly the way she did to me. *But wait, that was not my fault.* She did get me when I told her the reason I was there the first time, why not after that. I could not blame myself any longer. IT. WAS. NOT. MY. FAULT. People should quit assuming anything about me.

It was time I changed the narrative about why and what others do to me.

Given the rage, deep down, I knew if I wanted to be in control, I needed much more practice. Whatever else, I was an immigrant in the white Americans' eyes. This is a reality I would never be able to change. I could learn to deal with it more effectively.

It all came back to developing a strong voice to fight for myself.

From what I learned, social activism was a good environment for that.

* * *

I had been looking for volunteer opportunities in Bloomington. There were many out there but they had a waiting list of volunteers and they did not need me. After many months searching for the best suited organization, I found some work at the Education Outreach Office of Bloomington Hospital. I worked with a coordinator whose job was to provide information about Alzheimer and to organize its support groups for the community. I offered to do research and prepare new presentation materials for her, instead of sorting mails as she suggested. She welcomed the idea whole-heartedly.

In the end, I put together a power point presentation and co-presented it with the coordinator. Interactions with the community was a new source of lifeblood for me. It gave me the impression that I belonged in America.

But Alzheimer was not my passion. After one year, I moved on to the next activity at the Middle Way House, and the next.

For a few years, I felt so much involved in life and began to think there was a big chance I could truly become a part of this reality here in America.

One day at a local wine tasting party, I was in a conversation where people talked about capitalism and communism and Vietnam, Cuba and North Korea. A white American guy suddenly asked me where I was from. I said: "Originally, I come from Vietnam, but I actually am from Bloomington." I felt great to take control of the situation and established some ground rules with him about my ethnicity and citizenship. I believed I made it clear to him the way I wanted to be seen. Before I could even move my lips to make a social smile, he spurted out: "Which part? North Vietnam or South Vietnam?"

My blood started to boil as I detected exactly where the conversation was going. I knew some Vietnam veterans would sometimes ask me about specific locations in Vietnam to see whether that could be where they had been stationed in the war. This guy, from the way he talked about the Vietnam War earlier, I could smell he was still stuck in that timeline. Where on earth did he come from was the question I wanted to throw back at him. But I tried to play nice.

"Oh, no. The Vietnam War is a long-gone past. Vietnam is one country, an independent country where people are free to travel everywhere. People don't talk about North Vietnam or South Vietnam anymore. Not like the situation in North and South Korea."

"Oh, I see," he said. And blah-blah-blah.

Many Americans have a time machine or something. With just one question, they were able to transport me, without my permission, back to the previous century when Vietnam was a divided country. It is very annoying. Once again, I thought back about new strategies I needed to arm myself in social gatherings where many people were around and I certainly did not want to make a scene. I thought hard about how I tried to move forward when life around me kept me tied so much to things of the past. It made the present not very appealing. We were way past the 'Vietnam War' or the

'GIs and Asian prostitutes' area. I was not even a refugee or a boat person. I was none of those. I was not a usual immigrant either. I came to the U.S. as a graduate student on scholarship. Talking about that reminded me of the final 'reward' that capped my 'foreign student' experience in America. It was the climactic episode in a public health classroom.

We were learning about how health workers had to be in contact with people from diverse backgrounds and we needed to be sensitive about it. It was part of our job to recognize people as different individuals coming from different cultures.

In this class we happened to have quite an international student body representing many cultures: Chinese, Iranian, Japanese, Saudi Arabian, Thai, Vietnamese, Caucasian American, a combination of Spanish and Native American. We each tiptoed trying not to lump yellow with Asian culture, white with Western, and dark hairy with Arab. Appearances deceived, you know. Everything went great! Until the Japanese student gave her presentation.

Halfway through she needed a volunteer to do some yoga demonstrations for her health program. A few seconds passed and no one moved. The silence was so cold my hair on the neck began to stand up. I swore that I could hear the echoes in the collective mind of the class aiming at me. The Arabs thought I needed to volunteer to help the Japanese student because I was her Asian buddy. The Thai guy believed I should help because I was a girl. The Chinese woman thought the Vietnamese got along better with the Japanese than the Chinese, thus my inclination to help the presenter. The white Americans thought I should naturally want to help my fellow Asian gal because I seemed to be nice.

I was determined not to move a muscle to see what happened. Then, to my shock and surprise, the white girl sitting next to me whispered my name as a way of saying I should volunteer. The way she used her tone of voice and motioned her eyes, she told me that by not moving I actually committed two crimes: one of betrayal to my fellow tribe and the other of not conforming to the role assigned to me by the majority of whites. I sat still like a piece of stone pressing tight the lid that covered my rage.

Deep down, I thought even if I pulled together all the resourcefulness and wits I had with me, I still could not react constructively to a situation like this one.

Many incidents similar to this one have happened ever since. In fact, they were my daily life reality. More than ten years living in the U.S., I was still not prepared to deal with them as effectively as I wished. Do people really learn to, I wondered. Startled every time an issue of my ethnicity comes up, I find myself scavenging for words and ways of explaining. This coping and resistance energy was sipping away the juice of joy in my life. Sooner or later, I knew I would go berserk and turn so antisocial I'd hate who I had become. I needed to channel it into something positive.

* * *

I sat down to write. My articles in Vietnamese were published in the *Viễn Đông Daily News*. I kept the diacritics in my name. It was still a standard over here, and quite understandable, for English language mediums to type Vietnamese names without diacritics. In fact, the sight of Vietnamese names without accent marks used to be second nature to me—as a Western last name formerly represented a secret desire of a young girl yearning for power, as a blue-eyed blond-haired guy once symbolized a sacred dream of a forever happy marriage (like in the *Life* magazine add. Ha!). But I have learned that identity oscillations are in various places, sometimes as inconspicuous as the accent marks in the Vietnamese language. Without a doubt, the uniqueness of the Vietnamese language lies, among other things, in the diacritics. I even think that without diacritics, it is not Vietnamese. Now I wanted to keep that Vietnamese heritage the best way I could.

It is quite refreshing and rewarding to look at my Vietnamese name with diacritics on paper and online. I had found a prong to hook my identity on to fight for it. All the hassles I went through over time led me to this huge moment when eventually I was able to use my voice. Life can be unfair, but there is nothing much to *think* about. The best thing I could *do* is to use my voice to fight the battles of my choice. Action. I don't need to look anymore. I just do it.

It was more than just a Vietnamese last name with diacritics I kept. I re-acquired a piece of myself, renewed; I reactivated the original fighting power in me. The soft falling tone of the diacritical mark *dấu huyền* in my name served as a stick I put in the ground to mark my claim of territory. As it pierced the soil softened by the rain so did it sever my deep tie to the alienated desire for foreign-ness. The old source of nourishment was gone. I gulped up the unrelenting rainfall until I was washed clean of any dark soil that could stick to my skin. I am whole and happy as I was reborn, free of any ancestral and foreign sins that used to cause wrath in my days and nights. The tension of having to express and explain my Vietnamese identity within other people's framework evaporated. My writing is where I feel free to be who I am.

16. ACTION

I HAVE COME FULL CIRCLE. FINALLY, I am doing the very thing I have dreamed of. The early desire 'to do something about Vietnamese culture' materialized as it took a foothold and was on its way to blossoming. I am writing about Vietnamese people and culture, extending it with stories of my time as a Vietnamese American.

I set up a blog and published the English versions of the articles online. The publication of the English articles was a tremendous boost to my confidence because I relied on only myself to make it happen. There are some minor grammar and syntax mistakes here and there but they are nothing compared to the achievement of having my messages available for readers of both English and Vietnamese.

Every few articles, I stopped and asked myself whether I was satisfied with the direction I was going. The writing itself brings pure joy, but something was missing, still. A thousand-word article is too short to go deep and wide into discussing and sharing what I needed to. I am a Vietnamese American living in the U.S. I looked around, not many people have talked about, neither has there been enough written about, issues near and dear to my heart. Vietnamese Americans have already produced fictions and non-fictions in increasing number detailing their different journeys in American life. Their narratives filled up holes and inserted meaningful perspectives in all of us. Yet a sizable part of their themes sizzles around the Vietnam War and its related aspects. They cannot but sound alienated to me in many ways. I needed to forge my own part. Of the many things I considered overdue to resurface for air and scrutiny, even a few hundred newspaper articles would not bring me close to peeling off their layers to expose them.

Time is running out. A day goes by as I blink. I sit down to write, by the time I stand up for a break, the weekend has arrived. A season slices through faster than the time I take to recall the name of the previous season. Then it takes a few weeks to get used to signing the date with a new year. One more year has passed.

I could not wait for others to write the stories of my time. I needed a bigger project.

At the mark of my one-year writing 'career' in 2012, I began planning for a book. I was 40, not an early start for such a big project, but I did not mind at all. The beauty of life in America is that people believe anything is possible. I still do. There is nothing much to think about—I simply carried out the planned actions, one step at a time. There was only enough time for me to live my stories out loud, one at a time, one a day.

I began to record my friends as they told me stories about their lives. I interviewed my mom, my aunts and uncles for sagas about grandpas and grandmas.

Cam popped up as a word that stuck in my head and demanded a life of its own.

So I sat down to write.

To dig deep into myself, I needed to laugh at myself a little and to forgive me for whatever mistakes I made or thought I did. It was the only way to find peace.

I had promised myself not to quit ever again. So I sat down to write and gave what it took to follow through with the book.

Calmness, I then learned, was another important thing that I needed in my arsenal to pour out an intelligible narrative.

So were details and clarity.

It was all about going down memory lane and fishing out events to clarify, make myself understood, to be humble, to cleanse, to criticize, to pause, to be whole, to find peace within.

Quite predictably, I went to Vietnam looking for closure, reconciliation, reconnection, to be de-Americanized, re-Vietnamized, de-Vietnamized, re-Americanized—whatever it is my human soul needs to do to fulfill a binary mindset constantly on a quest for balance and meaning.

For my own salvation. I did it all.

17. STAYING

FROM ĐÀ NẴNG, MAI C. set foot in Sài Gòn in 1996. Overwhelmed was exactly how she felt. Sài Gòn was marvelous and mesmerizing in her eyes with so many high-rise buildings. "I'll be working in those buildings someday," she told herself. They represented something so beautiful. Throughout college years, they were her lighthouse.

During this time, Mai C. also pursued a second degree in English as a Second Language. This endeavor led her to one of the evening classes where I was a teacher.

Mai C. stood out from the crowd. Her desire to learn and her enthusiasm for life were unmatched. Only six years apart in age, and probably because we sensed in each other the shared quality of strong-mindedness and stubbornness, Mai C. and I hit it off in a modern hyphenated relationship of teacher-student-friend. We talked frankly and openly about everything, and critiqued each other often.

As I was teaching in Hồ Chí Minh city, I watched my young students grow up at the end of the twentieth and beginning of the twenty-first century into a different generation. I witnessed how high tech began to attract and distract them. Even though I was one of the first to use the internet to search for a scholarship in the U.S. at a time when not many thought about it, I did not grow up with technology. Nor did I really feel the pull of materials and the desire for high tech toys in me. Because of that I was curious about young people who started to develop a passion for an advanced lifestyle that transcended location, age and time.

Fast forward fifteen plus years. In 2012, high-rise buildings are no longer the 'goal' for Mai C. She is now a Marketing and Retail Manager for a cell phone company in Sài Gòn. She lives in a luxury apartment in District 7 where her home is equipped with a spacious garage. Switching to Sài-Gòn-real-estate mode of thinking, I could visualize the pretty costly picture of her place in comparison to mine. It is like comparing San Jose, California, with Bloomington, Indiana. Sài Gòn is one of the most expensive cities in the world. Right outside the door, Mai C. can take her daily leisure river walk to enjoy the breeze and the sight of organized living quarters and a clean environment. Without the need to move any muscles, from the windows of both her office and her apartment, sensational Sài Gòn is within her view.

When I visited Sài Gòn in 2012, I contacted her. "The city has changed a lot," Mai C. told me. "I'll pick you up for a ride to reacquaint you to Sài Gòn."

The day came. A usual sunny day in Sài Gòn. I was waiting when the bell rang. I opened the door to the sight of a dark grey Mercedes parked by the curve. Mai C. is the same, smiling and cheerful as always. The short curly hair does not age her a bit. Sporty as I remember her in jeans and t-shirt, she giggled and said 'Hi.' I also smiled and greeted her. Looking at and thinking about her car I was actually somewhat shocked and puzzled. Getting in a car in America is a reflex. Being in a private car in Vietnam the first time was a sensational pulley that zip-lined me down the childhood memory lane.

* * *

For those of us who were born after 1970, growing up in Sài Gòn in the late 70s and the 80s was an interesting time. My mom said that, right after the last Americans left Vietnam and the last helicopter on the rooftop of the U.S. Embassy whirled off, the chaos around the city was very quickly replaced by silence and space. Mountains of things in the warehouses disappeared in a few days. Hurdles of furniture and the tattered trail of miscellaneous things people left behind on the streets in their hurried flight out of the city vanished. Shops and stores were empty. Like magic, the old materialistic and chaotic world was gone.

I did not see those things with my own eyes because I was too small at three years old to be allowed outside the house during those days. By the time I was in first grade in 1978, the city landscape was as simple and still as our mind was innocent. There was nothing standing out or perking up for my eyes and mind to focus on, for stimulation or incitement. Nothing to grasp my attention, to attract or distract. Nothing to play and nothing to read. Absolutely nothing. My outside world were the quiet familiar roads between home and school punctured by the great hegemony of mono-colored plainness of heat and dirt. I don't remember a lot of trees, nor the colors. Just hot cement and hotter breeze. And an empty and heavy feeling of grayness.

There is one form of entertainment, completely free of charge, that I remember: hanging out with some older kids in the extended family and a few others in the neighborhood. We played games. Actually, as it was more likely that they considered me too small to be in the game, they would have excluded me from any team. But I followed them anyway. They ran, I ran. I don't remember what kind of hide-and-seek game they played but we chased one another throughout the tiny alleys to the nearby neighborhoods. From my house in Phú Nhuận district, without crossing any main street, using only these residential lanes and circles around my area, I could get to the Railroad Number Six and the Bùi Chu Catholic church neighborhoods in minutes. After a while, I lost the older kids because they were faster than me. I was alone to chase myself.

I passed many houses, most of them being multi-level, most of them having iron doors and iron fences. Many appeared to be very big and tall for a kid of seven, because I had to look up a lot of the time to see the flowers on the balcony. I tried to remember the detailed layout of the alleys. Where a house suddenly protruded, some sections became so narrow only two people maximum could fit at a time. Or the alley came to an abrupt L-turn and I had to slow down to avoid hitting my head into the brick wall. These markers made running around the alleys like discovering secret tunnels. The alleys took me to the main street, Lê Văn Sỹ. Its older name under the South Vietnamese regime was Trương Vĩnh Ký. From there I walked back home feeling so proud and excited to have gone out of my neighborhood to get to the world 'outside' and to have 'discovered' a short cut there.

A few years later, I went to the Ngô Sĩ Liên secondary school in Tân Bình district near the airport. The wildest journey I remember from that time was the bike ride in the afternoon heat with friends. From Phạm Văn Hai street, we headed northwest. Passing Hoàng Văn Thụ park, it began to get really quiet as we went deeper into Tân Sơn Nhất airport residential area. We turned into smaller roads and biked together in winding empty streets with a lot of trees around. It was like the countryside. Some of my friends lived here and we liked their yard, as well as the neighbors'. So we climbed some trees picking fungi bark for a class project, and leaves, flowers or fruits for fun, if any kinds of fruits were available. There was a lot of space in this area compared to downtown Sài Gòn in districts One and Three, or other populous districts such as Four, Five, and Phú Nhuận. Most of Bình Thạnh was like the countryside as well. Thủ Đức then was a rural town outside of Sài Gòn and districts Two and Seven were non-existent. Life was simple.

All I wanted was for my parents to have an easier life, and better education for myself. Imagination for anything bigger than that was very unrealistic. Besides, there was nothing out there I saw that I desired.

During this time, transportation was a true nightmare. Every time we travelled from Sài Gòn to Đà Lạt to visit grandma, it was like going through hell before reaching our destination. My mom needed to get some official travel document at her teaching school and used it to buy tickets four months in advance. When the day came, she and the four of us got up and went to the bus station at four in the morning. It was always the five of us because my dad stayed put in Sài Gòn to teach in the summer. A skinny woman and four bony little kids fit into a cyclo. Our luggage lay at the footrest. My mom and two of us sat properly on the front seat higher up, and the two smallest mounted on top of the luggage.

We always felt so sorry for the pedalers, especially the older ones, who had to push forward with all our weight. Therefore, we tried to pick younger ones. At the same time, we were aware that this was their means of living and being picked equated to having food on the table. And even though the thought was not a physical impediment for us to overcome, it gave us a moral and philosophical headache.

Other than that, it was an enjoyable ride in the early morning breeze beholding the pink sky and the city gradually waking up.

When the children grew a little bigger, we switched to using a motor-cyclo. It was bigger and faster, and there was no visible sign of 'exploitation' for us to bear. On the motor-cyclo, I imagined the ride to be quite a spectacle. The exploding roaring sound of it. The big fat tail of smoke it puffed in the air. That was not a very environmentally friendly scene and I felt embarrassed of it. I tried to hide behind my siblings as much I could, not wanting to draw the attention of the whole world towards me sitting on a vehicle that farted pollution. In reality, I don't think anybody then really cared about either the noise or the smoke.

At the bus station, it was first come first serve. We hoped to get the good seats in the front, at least one for my sister who suffered terrible carsickness.

The driver of the vehicle was like a King who got the last word in any matter. He usually had one to two assistants. Once in a while, they made us sit all the way in the back. My mom would appeal to the 'King's mercy' by pointing out the unpleasant miserable episode of vomiting that my sister would uncontrollably display in the back. The 'King' would then command his assistants to give us some seats at the front of the bus. When that happened, we would sigh with great relief. With the help of a lot of ointment, my sister would barely survive the drive.

The assistants' job was to make sure the King's needs were met—be it coffee or tea or cigarettes, check the passengers' tickets, arrange seating for everybody, and sort out luggage. 'Luggage' itself was worth a whole story. It could mean a woven bamboo basket of chickens or pigs. It could also mean a 40-pound nylon bag of rice, cauliflower, carrot, avocado or persimmon, depending on which way the bus was heading. Sometimes it was just things in a big black bag that did not reveal what was inside. Once I imagined it to be a kidnapped child.

Anything that could not stay in the storage space in the belly of the bus went to the roof. I was just glad that in a bus with no air-conditioning and all the windows open, we did not have to smell chicken poop.

The assistants' more important job was to get more passengers. When they spotted prospective ones from afar, the bus slowed down. The assistants would hinge on the opening front or back door calling out their destinations: "Dầu Giây, anyone?" "Bảo Lộc?" "Long Thành?" The city names varied depending on which direction the bus was taking. The desired passenger would wave their hand and the bus stopped. He or she got on. Picking up extra passengers was understandable, because in a time of scarcity, everybody needed extra income. Only that we, as the legitimate passengers, had to pay the price on many levels.

We had already bought the hard-earned paper tickets that paid for our seats. In order to take extra passengers, the assistant guys made us sit as close to each other as possible. On a bench for three, they crammed five. Along the aisle, they put low plastic stools for extra passengers leaving no space for walking. Literally, we were shoulder to shoulder and nobody could move. We were squeezed up for hours like that. Very skinny people with no fat or much flesh to buffer the contact.

The experience became more dramatic as I got older. The five of us were separated. That meant my sister would have a window seat on my left, and I had a stranger next to me on my right. During the bumpy ride we had no choice but to 'massage' our hip bones against each other in this hell of a ride rhymed by potholes. Every time the bus landed in one, I could hear the scrubbing sound of bone on bone in my head.

One time, I was seated next to a young man. Thank goodness he appeared to be a gentleman. He was as quiet as I was and seemed to be suffering the same dilemma. He was a man, nonetheless! Chicken pots or not, sitting that close to a stranger, a man for that matter, was already excruciatingly awkward. I was thirteen or fourteen. Innocent and ignorant as I was, it still took me years to get the image and the sound of the grinding out of my head!

It was a whole day trip from Sài Gòn to Đà Lạt sardined in the bus, to cover roughly 200 miles. We always got to grandma's house when it was already dark.

Throughout these trips, I often sat looking out the window and thought: "What is it like to be on the front seat, to have a whole view of the landscape on both sides of the road? I want *that*."

Before it happened I was gone from Vietnam. I missed completely the time when Vietnamese people were free and able to buy a car for their own use. I could not imagine what it was like to move from potholes to posh. As a tourist, I was back in my city cruising around in a taxi, in the back seat. It was still the 'second-hand view' of the outside. It was neither fun nor satisfying.

In Mai C.'s car it would be different. We could stop anytime, space and time alike. Looking at the car on the curve, I was excited about claiming the passenger seat in the front and 'first-hand view' of Sài Gòn. Currents of thoughts circled in my head. If I was to understand the present Vietnam and its people, I had to connect my bus experience to Mai C.'s dream car. The Mercedes before my eyes presented hoops to jump and leaps of faith to reach before I could fill the gaps in the air and in my mind about changes, reality, past and present, broken dreams and realized dreams, distance and future, to really enjoy the materialization of a luxury car with a friend of mine in the driver's seat as a proud owner.

There was so much to digest it might cause amnesia. I am a U.S. citizen. I own a car. I own a house. I may live in the most powerful country on earth. I may be familiar with a more civilized society. I may have more money than many in Vietnam. I may know better. I may not. I shouldn't assume; this did not bring about clarity and continuity for my visit. *What did I miss all these years?* Standing on the curve I wondered. *Is the changed country going to play any part in my future?* Trying to connect the dots, potholes to the hot black Benz, my mind was filled with questions and anxiety.

Then I was in the car. It was very clean inside, as it was supposed to be. The car is a luxurious object, a trophy lover, a status symbol, a prized possession more precious than a medal. It has to be clean. The day when a car becomes a tool to be messed up with, or extra space to trash, is not here yet. Mai C. was calm and confident in the driver's seat.

Through the windows, out there Sài Gòn was passing by, in the heat and the dust. The doors were well insulated, yet an insidiously guilty feeling was creeping in. The image of the shiny Mercedes pulling through the cloud of dust and thick heat was piercing its way into my heart. The incredible contrast between a hot Sài Gòn I saw outside the window and the cool feeling I had inside the air-conditioned car, representing two different worlds separated only by a thin door, was all too good-and-bad to bear. People were sweating on their motorbikes. Even if there was an accident out there, I was in here, safe and sound. The buffer of ample space alone was enough to make me feel privileged. Just like in the U.S., the more space the more privilege. On one hand, the stark difference between the haves and the have-nots presented undeniable moral qualms that made me uncomfortable. On the other hand, sitting comfortably in the car, I seemed to breathe in and out the floating "secretive" and "prestigious" particles in the air. After ten minutes, all I could think of was: "This must be how 007 feels whenever he is inside his own 'toys.'" To the young and successful people in Vietnam in the twenty-first century, possession of an expensive car translates to prestigious toys for the privileged.

I remember reading, when in the U.S., about the emergence of this prestigious class of Vietnamese in land. Some reporters, in disapproving tone, mock them as pricks, the morally perverted millennials or the iGen. I took days to think about how I wanted to process the information. It was no news that the newly rich usually wear their materialistic heart proudly on the sleeve. If this was everything I knew about these young people, I could not really say I understood them at all. Probably there were many of them who were all that shallow and superficial. For many others, there should be more in them to discover.

Feeling like a 007 in the car, I suddenly had a strange idea. Right now all around me, local people could hardly tell I am partially an outsider when I speak Vietnamese. This insider-outsider mix of wanderlust is an advantage I'm happy to use to take a spin on the statement about the millennials and the iGen: I wanted to get a glimpse of what the future Vietnam could be like via the eyes of its young masters. If we consider young people to be pillars of a society, they are supposed to be ahead of the game, or even ahead of their time. In this case, I might be the one to have to catch up with them, people like Mai C., or I may not need to do it at all. Either way, I learned. In order to understand them I need, as an observer, to readjust my perspective to look beyond the surface, the materialistic life they pursue, to read them on a deeper level. If there are no layers to peel, so be it. At least they deserve that much.

So I decided to dig deeper to decipher what Mai C. thought, saw and felt.

After half an hour in her car, perhaps I inhaled enough privileged atoms, I seemed to gain a bit of a new understanding of them. Many of these young professionals work in the communications or service industries where new discoveries and creations are made everyday. Now that we are able to produce whatever we can imagine, we all live in a world where the border between reality and imagination seems to have blurred. The blurring is more so for people like Mai C. whose lungs are exceptionally porous of prestigious particles and whose imagination uncurbed by regulations. "What an incredible world they live in!" I thought, being very excited about this trip with her.

We passed the city center and headed toward the section of town on the other side of the river. Mai C. told me our first destination was District Seven. At the end of the 1990s, Sài Gòn became overcrowded. Its population reached many millions more than the original city design was able to handle. The plan to expand the city and move office buildings as well as other facilities outside Sài Gòn was discussed in the media. District Seven was the first official addition and expansion in that plan. A new development brimming with green space, high-end shops, shining business sections, and organized living quarters, District Seven is its own community. In so many ways, it was the 'sweetheart' of the Sài Gòn dwellers who took pride in their entrepreneurship and pioneering championship—in other words, the spirit of the South and the Southerners, as they are known to possess. I had a chance to see a model apartment just before I left the country.

As we were rolling around, Mai C. told me about the project. "One thing I like the most about this development is that the developers kept their promise and commitment to green space," she said with apparent enthusiasm and intense gratification in her voice. "I wish a development like this one to become a model for standard construction in Vietnam."

At this point, I was supposed to tell Mai C. how impressive the District appeared to me. I tried to muster up some response, but to no avail. The American side in me was dominating. My first reaction was: nothing. I did not feel a thing. Tourists like me do not come to Vietnam to see luxurious shopping centers and clean symmetrical asphalt roads, even when some shopping malls in Vietnam are actually brighter and shinier than many in the U.S. Clean, neat roads are my everyday sight in America. I came to Vietnam to look for things I could not see in the U.S.

I was not really a tourist through and through because I grew up here. Arriving in Sài Gòn for only a few days, I could not rub off the American mentality and perspective in me just yet. As Mai C. was talking, it struck me that once in Vietnam, I had to readjust and give myself up to a Vietnamese reality. I paused and pondered. Organization was my reality in the U.S., but definitely not one of the Vietnamese people's. I was here a long time back and I remembered that now.

The re-processed thought made me see that District Seven is, indeed, a prized and proud production of the Sài Gòn think tank, entrepreneurs and city dwellers who have tried tirelessly to revamp the avant-garde spirit of the South in the name of freedom and democracy. So many times cheated and betrayed by different forces with different agendas, all leaving behind a trail of unfulfilled promises, Sài Gòn residents are now happy to show outsiders that District Seven is living proof that it is still possible to rebuild the country as long as promises are kept. In this neat living space, "law and order are kept and maintained, and civilization established," Mai C. specifically told me. "The residents feel very safe here. They have their own regulations and rules of living. Their residential rights are protected here." As if to say a chance of revitalization is here to stay, I thought to myself.

So I did not respond to Mai C. accordingly right away but at least I understood where she stands. As one who works very hard to improve her life and contribute the best to the society, Mai C.'s main concerns are very practical: green space, law and order, safety and rights. The then-me when I lived in Sài Gòn desired the same thing. If I had not left for the U.S., I would still wish for those same basic things for my country and my people.

The historical connection and commentary about District Seven is my addition. My alluding to the Vietnam War by mentioning South Vietnam, freedom and democracy, and broken promises implying history has to be dealt with properly is very much an American/Western way of thinking, something I picked up after many years living in the U.S. This is the very lens through which the American tourist side in me brought to view Vietnam. It is not necessarily the way Vietnamese people see their reality.

For the purpose of deciphering Mai C.'s viewpoint, I should separate this insider-outsider mixture in my observation in order to see things in the right perspective. "If you have crawled on the dirt floor for food, you'd learn to appreciate a clean table and a chair before you understand what it takes to climb into an airplane. Things usually evolve step by step, except the exceptions," the insider-me reminded. "Agreed," the outsider-me admitted, "the essential thing to learn is to understand what comes first and what comes next. It is not that the Vietnamese don't care about history (this will be discussed more later by the insider-me). It is all about the Vietnamese priority." Not meaning to speak for Mai C., I try to understand how she operates by pitting my reactions and responses against hers on the backsplash of the now-me versus the then-me, or the insider-me versus the outsider-me to fret out some clarity.

So far being profuse in observation and scanty in compliments to Mai C. during her tour guide, I managed to make up as we went along: "It's very nice!" "Really! That's wonderful!" as we zoomed in and out of small parks.

It was almost noon. We were driving to the district center. I was suddenly not sure what time and space I occupied. I was in a car, talking and mixing Vietnamese with English. Everything around me was clean and neat. The restaurants had foreign names. When we got to the Crescent Pond, the center of attraction for residents, and so named because of its half-moon shape, I got out of the car and looked around. The shining buildings around me with huge glass windows from top to bottom curved in parallel to the pond. It was one very nice and curvy space. I saw the names of American business establishments above the office doors. The whole area looked just like a new development in the U.S. This could be the U.S.

I walked around and took pictures. Mai C. gave me space and time to do that. The sense of pride and confidence on her face was unmistakable. I took more pictures of the curvy glass building. The strange feeling only left and returned me to reality when we drove around the villas' area. These mansions could cost as much as half a million dollars. Stately looking, the multi-level houses are camouflaged by lots of trees, giving the residents optimal privacy. The yard around the house was rich with shapes, sizes, colors and dimensions. Short and tall, big and small trees. Neat rows of plants along the gates. Meticulously trimmed trees in the middle of the garden. Big trees near the house reaching to the balcony. Red and yellow flowers. Trees with big and small leaves. Purple hanging flowers. Bonsais. There were so many trees and the whole place was so green. They combined to create many layers of multi-dimensional pictures hiding the house inside like a gem. Right outside the gates, all the roads were so straight and smooth. I could hear a pin drop. A perfect mix of modernity and countryside serenity. It is so strange, yet so Vietnam.

Then it dawned on me that the confusion of time and space is within myself at moments of crossing borders, various kinds of borders, whether I am aware of it or not. I never thought about Vietnam as a salad bowl the way the U.S. is, but it is. The difference is that the mixture attribute is deep within each Vietnamese. A plethora of forces have encroached upon the geographical lines and memory slices of the country forcing the people to deal with them. They germinate their seeds in the populace. Adaptation seed has become a strong suit of each Vietnamese. They incorporate everything, from China, the USSR, Russia, Japan, the U.S. Nowadays in the time of globalization, the influence could be from anywhere, South Korea, Singapore, Spain, etc. The trait is visible and audible everywhere. There is always a sense of strangeness or foreignness in one way or another in the land. The outsider-me could detect and analyze the blending line, the insider-me lived it.

I did not know if Mai C. experienced the time and space confusion. She has travelled abroad quite a bit but has lived all her life in Vietnam. She might do it in a different way. She might not think of the mixture as confusion of time and space the way I do. She breathes it on a daily basis as a part of herself. Maybe it still is in the now-me, in spite of my efforts to change, just enough to spook me someday at the most unexpected moment. For what it's worth, the same adaptive trait that we share worked the same way pushing her to move forward in Vietnam. She was one person who could tell me everything I wanted to know about young people in Vietnam. She grew up with them, worked with them and now led them.

I needed to stick to her to infiltrate further her world slowly as a friend.

* * *

After ten days, I began to get used to the heat. I even appreciated the humidity because that meant I didn't need to lotion myself like in the U.S. One less thing to worry about. I thought with the humid weather in Vietnam one can beat one branch of product out of a corporation. But I was wrong. Body lotions, hand lotions, foot lotions are all over the supermarket shelves. The sound of growth and business opportunities in Sài Gòn was even more deafening than before. The power to make young and old and middle-age happy consumers buy, even a thing they don't ever need, is one trademark of globalization. One can find much more junk here, just like in the U.S.

The second time we hung around, "Let's go for a drive," Mai C. said. "There is this cute area I want to show you." "Where is it?" I asked. "Not far. It is one of the new hubs in Sài Gòn where expats gathered," she told me. From downtown Sài Gòn in District One, we headed toward the river. On the other side of the Sài Gòn bridge, there are new areas revamped totally when the city decided to expand its perimeter to include the surrounding areas. New roads, overhead walkways, and bridges opened up used-to-be grottoes and brightened them up with neon-lighted restaurants and clubs. They added quirkiness and diversity to the classic look of the city center creating still another aspect of welcoming mongrel(real)ity.

Getting off the noisy streets, we swung into more quiet areas of expat residences. The sun was going down. That did not deflect the solid armory-looking of the high-walled and high-gated houses gleaming with visible luxury. By the look of them, these houses were probably well-built and ensheathed by privacy and comfort for their residents. Clustering around these houses were clubby-looking restaurants that I imagined were patronized mainly by expats and professionals like Mai C.

I knew she spent her free time rummaging the old and new quarters recording changes to the face of Sài Gòn. After more than ten years away, I did not know Sài Gòn any more with all its new nooks and crannies. I suddenly felt missing Sài Gòn a lot, especially the ownership feeling that I had over the place where I grew up. I missed moments when I could just roam around small alleys and absorb the air ever changing its every atom by the second, no matter how stifling I thought it was. I lost the chance to stake my little piece of ownership on the new face of this city, and now it is gone. It belongs to expats and backpack tourists who scrounge every corner of the city for the best deal of their lives, and to youngsters who are busy acquiring a trinket of cool exotic mementoes and gadgets from all sources possible. Sài Gòn is Mai C.'s city, no longer mine.

At the end of the tour, Mai C. said she had reserved a table for us at a restaurant. To get there, we turned left and right into small alleys entering what looked like an old section of the city. These alleys were definitely not made for cars. In my estimation, there was only enough space for one car to go. As we got deeper into the lane near the restaurant, there was another car coming out from the opposite direction. I was jumping on my seat thinking we had to back out all the way to make space for the other car. Mai C. was cool as a cucumber next to me. She pulled her car close to the wall on her right and stopped, while a guide appeared out of the blue to help the other driver navigate the tight squeeze out. I was amazed. The squeezing stunt in Sài Gòn was as fascinating as the way people in Bangkok would park in a small garage, leaving their car in neutral so that others can push it back and forth to make needed space to get their car out. Now I thought Asian people were really dexterous.

Then it was Mai C.'s turn to be guided to park in the tiny designated space.

We got out of the car and headed toward the restaurant. As we walked through the big glass doors with fancy shining stainless steel handles, a hostess approached. Mai C. promptly declared her name, "Mai C." "Right this way," the hostess nodded and motioned her hand to show us. She responded in English! I was almost shocked but did not say anything because, once inside, I noticed that I must be the oldest person here. I knew I entered a different world.

I trod my way cautiously, envying the young patrons their secure manner that seemed to say they 'owned' this place. The hostess set us up at a table by the water. We were on the deck right over the Sài Gòn river.

Vietnamese people are fascinated with running water, be it the ocean, a river, waterfalls, or creeks, as much as the Germans take pride in their mountains and forests, as much as the Swedish love the lakes. As a result, a table right by the water, or better yet, over the water where you can literally see it flowing underneath your feet, is prime seating coveted by all clients of the restaurant.

So there we were settling down at our spot. The hostess brought over the menus. We ordered drinks and then food. We were all speaking English. I was very confused by the fact that Vietnamese people spoke English as if it was some kind of a second official language. At first, I thought it could be a trend for young professional Vietnamese to speak English in fancy places because they could and to show off. If this was the case, it was a bizarre thing to do for pretentious and obnoxious people. Many young wealthy people were all that and I would not be surprised by it. Yet, before I could get a hang of what was really going on, my mind was immediately occupied by a second thought more worrisome.

Remember that I grew up in the post War era; an American or Western presence, except the Russians, was unheard of until much later. Normal city topography was an unmatched hegemony of communist law and order. At the end of the century, Vietnamese economic sputtering caught the attention of the world. American companies became a favorable presence in Vietnam and financial prosperity in Sài Gòn a dream to the countryside folks. I was pleased with the many changes. At the same time, I did not think the country should slip back into a mediocre new version of the Vietnam War-American GIs-prostitutes-broken English-reality show.

As I was sitting here in semi-darkness listening to an Asian hostess speaking English in a club-like restaurant, some very notorious images of the Vietnam War flashed before my eyes. My

heart was throbbing anxiously. "Hang on," the insider-me interrupted. "Did you dare to raise in mind a speckle of doubt towards
the young masters thinking they could sink to that bottom? Your
association of this fancy place to a Vietnam War reference is so
revealing of your American/Western thinking. The then-you and
the insider-you know better than this. Tell me, why Americans
or people who do not live in Vietnam are so obsessive about the
Vietnam War. They often come to the country for a visit and walk
away with what they consider a revelation about the post-war country and its people: 'Young Vietnamese these days know nothing
about the Vietnam War because they are too busy catching up with
capitalism.' You cannot come to a café or walk along the street, talk
to a youngster or two, and conclude that they don't know anything
about history. And why do they have to know about the specific
Vietnam War more than any other wars in their history? Ask any
youth in the world these days what they care about, their country's
history or the new iPhone! It is global youth culture! Most youngsters care about themselves and the new gadgets! It's globalization!"

That is true. The now-me stopped the passing thought. There
was nothing in this situation to suggest such a low moral Vietnam
War reality when all three of us were Asian women, we dressed
nicely, we spoke perfect English, and there was no white guy involved. Back when I was younger, whenever I thought about all
the wars that happened in my country, I wanted to forget them all.
Thinking about them only compounded the repression I had to
handle and made life more suffocating. I had heard about boat people and the sorrowful tales of the survivors as a legacy of war. But
there is always unfinished business after a war. To be just to everybody, does that mean we have to go back and deal with the Chinese,
the French, the Japanese, the Cham, the Koreans, the Cambodians,
the Americans? What does that even mean and whose responsibility is that?

Between negotiating and fighting the obligations to family,
resisting social pressures and outdated expectations of women,
catching up with the changes, dealing with corruptions while

remaining true to oneself, learning to protect oneself, and fighting the decomposing of Vietnamese society in full putrefaction, I had more than a handful. Being forgiving, even forgetful, and being practical go a long way. I was like that. I now see that in Mai C. and people in Vietnam. They aim for the best with what they are dealt with. Forget the American/Western patronization, young Vietnamese these days are working very hard trying to catch up with the world.

For what seemed to be a long moment I was caught up in my thoughts, Mai C. was on my left calm and confident. The whole her was right here. Relaxed. Me: Tensed as I still was, I turned to the hostess. She looked Asian and could be Vietnamese. Not wanting to be offensive in any way by asking a silly question such as "Are you Vietnamese?" to a Vietnamese, at the same time trying not to assume anything, I asked the hostess: "Do you speak Vietnamese?" "No, I am Singaporean," she replied. She carried herself very professionally. Here in this deck restaurant, it could be bizarre but obviously it did not look and sound like a historical nightmare I was worried about a moment earlier. I calmed down.

In my own experience visiting Vietnam the past years, I have been to Vietnamese hotels managed by an American or a Thai corporation. Now I realized the time for a small high-end restaurant to hire a foreign manager has arrived, and that it has even become a norm in the Vietnamese small business scene. Mai C. later confirmed this reality to me. Still, I found it problematic. The restaurant was definitely exclusive for English speakers only. The linguistic discrimination was a clear demonstration of a visible gap between the rich and the poor in the country that rich people daringly displayed. As bad as it was from the liberal point of view, this uneven distribution of wealth is inevitable in social development in every nation, and glaringly so in the U.S., the UK or China today. Dwelling upon it this moment does not do me any good. I had to let it slide to focus on other things.

In a way I was not surprised at the linguistic frenzy in Vietnam. Besides the fact that Vietnamese people aim to garner management skills from the foreign experts, nowhere in the world are people more passionate about learning English than in Vietnam. It is one effective tool to climb the social ladder and change one's status. Well-off families in post-war Vietnam, more than twenty years ago, began to send their children to international schools within the country, mostly in Sài Gòn and Hà Nội, so the kids would be fluent in English upon college graduation. The advantage in English language skill will definitely help them secure a good job.

In the twenty-first century, another schooling trend started with parents managing to send their children abroad for high school and college. I personally witness enough, both in the U.S. and Vietnam, to say that I am expecting to see a new generation of bilingual Vietnamese who are much more diverse than we used to be.

It was nervous, scary, and extraordinary all the same, to see that once again, Vietnam is in the forefront of change. In peace, with free will and being presented with choices, Vietnamese people choose to diversify. They go everywhere around the globe, not just to study, but to get married, to work, to travel, to find an alternative reality, just like people on earth have been doing all along. This time, they come back, a lot of times with more than just themselves. The bridge from and to Vietnam is maintained, Vietnamese reality is getting complicated. Mixed race Vietnamese, or people with very diverse backgrounds, being a part of life in Vietnam will become a huge show some day, if it not already is.

I did not have to look very far.

On the table next to mine, two very young men were drinking some good-looking colorful drinks, and talking in English. I recognized a Caucasian guy. The other one was more tricky. He could be a Singaporean, a Korean, a newly naturalized Vietnamese American, or a Vietnamese who went to international school all his life. It is difficult to describe his appearance. His looks are meticulous yet unfiltered, modern yet unoriginal, Asian yet universal. It appeared as a desperate and restless effort to compile and devour anything modern. This is how I perceive many 'updated' young people to look like these days everywhere, especially in large numbers in Asia. They don't bear nationalism or a clear ethnicity. They cross many borders.

Right now in front of my eyes were two generations of young Vietnamese, Mai C.'s and her younger sibling's. The latter needed more time to grow and to catch up. My priority was to observe the first. I thought it was time I focused on my dialogue with my friend.

Mai C. asked me a lot of questions. In fact, she was one of a few who asked me that many questions about my life in the U.S. Ever since I arrived to Vietnam, I noticed that whenever I talked to my relatives and old friends, I had to do all the talking and ask all the questions. On one hand, I did have a need to catch up with life in Vietnam, thus my questions. On the other hand, I had the feeling that people did not know what questions to ask me as if they heard so much about the U.S. already they knew all the answers. More importantly, all the conversationalists I faced seemed to have a huge urge to be listened to. I asked one question and they started to pour out.

With Mai C. it was different. I tried to dodge her questions so that I could get to her story. I already told her I wanted to collect material for my book about Vietnam and that I would like to record our conversation. OK, she said. Now that we were immobile in a restaurant I thought it was a good chance to turn on the recorder.

I began to ask her a lot of questions. After half an hour I felt awash as if there was nothing else I needed from her. At the same time, I felt this urge for additional questions as if insatiable for more I had to go on. I followed my gut and carried this through. All along I was expecting some magical moment to happen, just because our meeting again after ten years was incredible, or because I thought she was an incredible person, or both. Did it happen but somehow I missed it, I was not sure. I may have been distracted thus missing the moment. This could be true. Or it may not have happened and I only tricked my mind. I simply knew that I was left with suspense and some emptiness on my part.

At this point during dinner, a drilling machine went on.

There was construction at the building next door. The workers must have felt that the coolness after sundown was a perfect time to work. The tick-a-tack grumping from the drill machine ate all our words. I may have lost the magic moment to the noise. Or, the magic I hoped to catch could be as illusive, even deceptive, as a new electronic gadget one has in hand. One moment one feels the whole world is within reach, the next moment it is emptiness that prevails. I often felt the same about stories of successful young Vietnamese professionals, about how much money they make and how they spend it, and about the privileges in life they buy for themselves. The stories are full and empty, rich and hollow at the same time. And, sometimes from the mouth of adults their stories sound as simple and typical as kids' stories. Yet, for the sake of my peep into a Vietnamese future, I could not afford to forget that Mai C. and her peers are the twenty-first century kids. High tech is their reality and I needed to catch them at moments the world was in their hand, not when it glided through.

I tried to speak their language and listened to them talk.

In their own words, they emit deep waves of aspiration and inspiration for a life camouflaged by stages of hi-tech toys. The toys that surround them are laying the bridge to the next higher 'extraterrestrial' journey. In this futuristic environment, the magical moment I expected to happen between us meant no more than a reconnection I hoped to make to the shared past we had together where we were patrons of the then Vietnamese future. It was gone the second I left the country. I should let it go to focus on the new moment, to create a new connection as a guest.

The minute I let go of my self to embrace the new force of the future, I understood another aspect of the loss I felt at the end of my conversation with Mai C.—as someone who left, I simply could not add anything to the story of one who knew exactly what she wanted and how to get there, living in a place she called motherland. Without borrowing any lens to frame the responses, I let them flow. The determination and sharpness of her mind, and the wisdom she possessed squared off her story neatly on the page.

Have your needs changed now that you have a lot of money?
'Change' may not be a precise word. It is only human nature that the

more you have the more you want. Once you have A, you move on to B. Looked closely, A is in fact simply a door to reveal what is behind it. The more we can see what is behind A, the more we know how to sharpen what we want. Therefore, if one does not have a chance to pierce A, one does not really know what they want. Many people live their whole life without knowing what they really want. I think I am lucky to 'see' a lot and to know well what I want.

So what do you want? I want to work on different areas in various departments in different companies, so I can learn the most I can. After that, I want to see my role in the company enlarged. Then, of course, the chance to run my own company. By this time, with the experience and maturity from work, plus the established networks, I could 'see' the opportunities out there and more importantly, I could seize them. I have to say the best place for one to 'see' the opportunities out there is in the corporations. They are the hub of information, the centers of resources, personnel, ideas and new inventions. Access to them means access to opportunities.

Do you aim to make a lot of money? Who doesn't want a lot of money! I want to make a lot of money, but that is not my goal. I want to have a career. I believe that promotions in a job equal more money. Still, money is not the destination. In the end, I work because of my passion and beliefs in what I am doing.

What is your goal in the present time? Advance and Ahead. To catch up with all the new trends. Communications change very quickly. It is digital today, it could be something different tomorrow. If you cannot keep up and update yourself fast enough you become outdated like so many others. Once you choose communications, you cannot stop. To stop means to be backward. The winner in this game is one who can advance and stay ahead, and with good networks.

Are passion and ideals important to you? Passion certainly is. Ideals: they are the ability to carry out the passion, instead of something lofty I used to think about. Ideal is to be able to do what you like that not only can provide for you but also raise you to first-class citizen. I am not talking about passion like an artist, but passion here is just the ability to do what you want and what you believe in.

The most simple 'want' for my generation is financial freedom and being updated. Passion in this case leans towards financial calculations therefore it simultaneously brings you a very comfortable life. It is only a means that once reached you are financially free and can improve the quality of your life tremendously. If you have to work so hard all day long just to make ends meet, that is miserable. Is that pragmatic, I'd say practical. These days, to say that you are capable means you can afford a comfortable life. Our society is now pretty fair in terms of how much effort you invest in your job and the results you get from it. It is not like the old days.

What is your joy in life? *Achievements in work make me happy. I manage to balance my life and I enjoy life. I refuse a pitiful and lonely life. I like to explore and therefore my life is very interesting.*

How about your friends? *To this point, friends are part of the adaptation process. Once you have a new group of friends who fit better with your job, your point of view, your time, your schedule, in other words the culture you are in, the old ones drop out of the scene gradually.*

With a lot more money, do your values in life change? *Not really. The most important thing to me unchanged over time is still human relations. To care for and love others in life. That is important to me.*

In your opinion, what are the challenges of the 21st century for Vietnam? *For me, economic and political stability in the country and the region is the main concern because it is out of my control but affects directly the domestic micro-economic situation and the people's life. Other than that, human resource is a challenge as the issue of training for the next generations in Vietnam is not adequate and will lead to negative consequences.*

What do you think about dreams in life and do you have many left to fulfill? *When I was small, when asked about dreams, I often said that I wanted to become a doctor or a teacher. When I was older, I thought being a doctor or a teacher did not bring prosperity to my country. As an adult like I am now, I just want to contribute to building a strong Vietnam with my part of the job. I want my loved ones* *to be healthy and happy. These days in Vietnam, we talk a lot about young people who are confused and narcissistic. I just think if people were better-off and suffered less financial pressure, coupled with better education, they would live in harmony and be more civilized. I dream of that worthy life right here in my homeland.*

* * *

In the past ten years, Mai C. has been busy fulfilling her dreams. She established and ran her own company for nearly ten years. At almost the same time she held a directorship position in another foreign company continuing to expand her expertise in research and marketing consumer products for Vietnamese market. She has traveled the world admiring the Taj Mahal in India, the pyramids in Egypt, and the Great Wall in China; climbing the Corcovado mountain and walking the Copacabana beach in Brazil; cheering life in Melbourne, Sydney and Tasmania in Australia; feeling lost to the universe at Cape of Good Hope in South Africa; submerging in nature in Phuket and Chiangmai in Thailand and Bali in Indonesia; pondering Taiwan, Hong Kong, Singapore and Malaysia as the four Asian dragons. Once a factual far-fetched dream, traveling has become a tool and means to reach a gratifying life for people like Mai C. and her generation.

I envy the fact that they are living many of their dreams right in their homeland. They are staying. And they are building their country. People like them who work hard for their dreams are the core of a nation. Not me, not anyone who left nor anyone who is now standing looking in. They are the young masters, after all.

"Isn't it an optimistic picture of Vietnam you have?" the then-me insider-me quizzed. "Did your friend's practicality make you forget the everyday oppressive environment in Vietnam you once ran away from? Or the degrading educational system?" she mocked. "Not at all," the outsider-me confirmed. "It is because I was out, I now have a chance for second thoughts. Yes, corruption on a small scale in Vietnam is more prevalent than in many parts of the world, and repression deplorable. But these corrupted individuals can be dealt with. For example, a whole class can stand up against a corrupted teacher. A whole department can confront a self-serving chair. Every single citizen can resist bribing a traffic police officer. And so on. I know, it is easy for me to say. What if you stand up to corrupted people and they attack you for revenge or use intimidation on you? What if you get arrested and jailed? Who takes care of your family?

"I'd say more than half the population have to be committed to being a part of change for real change to happen. Start with small things like those mentioned above. Like, staying in line to wait for one's turn instead of cutting the line; don't trash the public places; don't steal a neighbor's plants at night; don't steal books from a free neighborhood library. Life already becomes a little easier and more pleasant with these courtesies. Agreeing to commit good deeds on little issues means people share the same pride and honor. It means they are more willing to stand together for a bigger cause. For more serious issues, somebody has to pick up the fight. Many Vietnamese activists have been and are doing that. They speak the truth and go to jail. Their actions mean activism and sacrifice. Things are changing.

"At the same time, as an outsider, I have learned things I wish I had in the old days. I learn that people can use democracy or patriotism as a label to raise a war on others, a manhunt for the benefit of a few. Very soon, any concept can be pushed to an extreme and used to haul up control on the hands of a few. I learn to be careful with everything I see and read out there. I learn not to curse my government in vain; each citizen has to take some action to fight for what they believe in. That is what the people in each country have to do. In the case of Vietnam, we may wish that outsiders just leave us alone so we would find a way to solve our problems among ourselves.

"OK, I am one who left. I don't live here. I have no rights to meddle in any way. I feel like a coward. I should shut up now. I agree."

* * *

So many things have gone awfully wrong in Vietnam under the current government. Pretty much the same things happened with the government before that, and before that, and before that. No government on earth is free from flaws. According to Keith W. Taylor, the Vietnamese people have tried out and failed many experiments in management. I agree with him that they will certainly continue to try more. I have learned to bypass the name or the hat that Vietnamese people wear and the changing element of the -ism underneath, to focus on the unchanging part: The people and the land stay. Whatever happens, or doesn't happen, communism or post-communism or what's-in-a-name-ism, my only wish is that the people in Vietnam choose these specific battles to fight for, the same battles I signed up for: equality, human rights, justice and freedom, no matter how relative their meanings are.

What I can do is to have hope for Vietnam. I think about the present and the future. As passion drives life forward, as people who stay behind are those who are actually building the country, as determination and risk-taking propel people in life, so I believe that those like Mai C. represent one possible future of Vietnam. It is an alternative to one that foreigners normally projected in support of a blue-blooded individual who came from a well-connected family.

But it is also easy to see that they can work together towards a shared future.

Then there is an issue with modeling after an ancient or a new country. In an 'ancient' country where old money is abundant and style is overflowing, social mobility is very much determined by the bloodline, connections, or the old-boy system. In a new country, anything can happen. America embodies the dream of so many people around the world because it is a new country where people know they can always make a fresh start. Vietnamese and people around the globe still look to America as a beacon on a hill. I can still see a large part of America as a new country, but it is only wise to remember that coming to the twenty-first century, as I was typing these words, America is getting old.

Vietnam has been reborn so many times throughout its history. After each war fought and won, its blood is filtered. After each new political ally acquired or an old one reacquainted, new blood cells are created. Being relatively in peace for the longest time ever since the late twentieth century, the Vietnamese blood is refreshed over and over after each political adjustment is made to achieve equilibrium in the regional arena and to make itself a little more visible in the world ring. More than ever, with increasing new blood of 21C from a diverse population of young people, Vietnam could be reborn again sometime soon. Whether it will follow the path of an 'old' or a 'new' country is difficult to tell. Once again, Vietnam won the initial battle against the spread of COVID-19 pandemic in early 2020 shocking its own citizens and the developed countries. Maybe being the master of mongrel-ity as they are, they will etch out a new path for themselves. I surely hope so.

18. HOME

EMPTY PLATES. FOOD STAINED SILVERWARE. Half-full wine glasses. Candlelight. The talking around the table was nothing out of the ordinary. Just a dinner. I was rehearsing in my mind and looking for the right moment to make a comment to confront my guests. Then I aborted the thought.

As a U.S. citizen, my home is Bloomington, Indiana.

But if America is home, how come I cannot bring myself to say: "We Americans have made a mess with the 2016 election. Our country is in deep trouble"? Now, in writing, it looks OK. But the sound of 'we Americans' coming from a petite black hair flat nose yellow skin totally Asian looking me could be bizarre. It could provoke rage. 'We Americans' with me being an American citizen, included, does not sound right to many ears. I did try to put 'we' referring to us all Americans in a rainbow of skin colors in my sentence a few times before, and some of my white audience just ignored what they heard. It is better that they pretend not to hear it than to react to it unfavorably, I guess.

It is reassuring for them to hear me say 'us' meaning Vietnamese and Vietnamese Americans. This way we Vietnamese and Vietnamese Americans remain 'the others' and they know I am not encroaching their space. It is easier for them to deal with me when they know I know my place, I guess. Do I belong to the same place they do? Am I the same 'us' to them? I very much doubt that.

What is my place, I am not sure. In America, besides the fact that it is illegal to exclude me as non-American (but who cares about legality, it is the unrevealed thoughts and unchallenged actions that destroy), the revolting feeling I have about claiming some place as home causes uncertainty. The queasiness may come from me not being able to figure out how to be a Vietnamese and a Vietnamese American the way I am expected to be. I refuse to play any game.

19. ONE

4O COULD NOT BE BETTER than this. I looked at myself in the mirror, touched my cheek and was surprised and amazed at the smoothness of the skin. I looked and felt like a twenty-year-old.

I visited Vietnam again.

A week earlier, I had walked out of Tân Sơn Nhất airport in Sài Gòn. Through the last door, the air conditioning was no more. A wave of tropical heat engulfed me. Immediately it felt almost un-bearable and un-breathable. The hot air was so thick. It enveloped me in the total impact of the noises, movements, chaos, and fluc-tuations of human emotions.

People scurry around looking for people, looking for taxis. Some look happy, some exhausted, some cranky, some unemo-tional, others competitive, still others suspicious. People are carrying things, a lot of things, pulling a big cart on which suitcases and carton boxes mounted up to their chin. I know these people. I know what their facial expressions mean. I understand the nuances in their tone of voice and body gestures. In each of them, I see a story in itself of a life so raw I hardly have a chance to witness in America, especially in a college town such as Bloomington where the school of music activities are so rich. Then, as if I was swim-ming in the raw honey dripping off the beehives, golden chunks of it, breaking to pieces, shining in the sun, I found myself submerged in this emotion-all-atmosphere. In spite of the total impact of the incredible noises surrounding me, I could detect the movements of everything and also the fluctuation in people operating with emotions at instinctive levels.

Actually, something had happened before all the detective thoughts came to mind. The moment the heat wave enveloped me, my body was absorbing every tiny particle of humidity with a vengeance. It responded to the humidity the way the stranded fish on shallow water would react when it was released back into deep water. I considered it the fascination of the motherland. My body already knew what took my mind seconds to realize. I was home.

With it, deep inside, some comfort set in. Humidity was comfort. It smoothed out wrinkles and restored youthfulness.

I was back in Sài Gòn, the hometown where I grew up. After more than ten years living in the U.S., I now had a chance to look at my own country from an extra point of view.

After the initial shock subsided, I looked around and shivered to realize how beautiful Vietnam is. It truly is. Most of the time, you would not find anything like Yellowstone, Bryce Canyon, or Mall of America—things on a big scale the way they are in America. Instead, a unique way of combining colors and shapes and sizes in these houses and those little shops and cafes, and the sensuous green spotted in unexpected places around the city make you feel easily at home, from the first time you see them. Intimacy culture is the term I called it. Things and people present and the atmosphere created are not to impress you, but to invite you in.

A friend reminded me that maybe not everyone could afford to think about the kind of beauty and optimism I talked about. True. It does not matter where I go, life, for many people, starts with the most basic.

In this huge country of almost a hundred million souls, visitors will surely find whatever they want to find. But in the end, it's all about the people—visitors would tell you so as they describe it as one of the best things about traveling to Vietnam. One of my favorites was the *xe ôm* drivers. Their stories were so raw-ful-ly honest they gave me chills.

On the back of his motorbike, his lifeblood, I listened to Đạt as he told me about the newly formed profession for drivers like him. Everyday, he would drive his child clients back and forth between home and school. In between, he delivers goods for some local merchants, takes his regulars to the airport, or goes to buy a big flowerpot with another client. It was a tight network of local people and businesses. Entrusting in him the safety of their children and their business, the parents, the clients and the drivers became each other's people. Daily survival matters have not changed for centuries for many people as they live one day at a time.

I saw my grandma in their stories. I saw myself in them. A version of us. The original version of a common everyday life shared by most human beings on earth. Governments turn their back on them. Their only hope is themselves and individuals like them who care.

Life, for many people, does not change in a hundred years. Many of us choose and strive to divert from here to park on more elevated ground. Yet this is still the place where we all come back to someday, with our philanthropy project, to use the most noble term of all to call it, or with our charity program, to use a down-to-earth type of vocabulary to describe it, to 'help' them—being afraid to admit to ourselves that we are back here to relocate and refill with a source of life strokes and commonsense and wisdom that are profound and vivacious enough they help push us back on our feet in our modern advanced life.

I know some spot of life is fragile and sacred territory. So I tread lightly. Or else.

But I don't forget that Vietnam could be huge, in a different way, the Western way, these days.

Hà Nội is the capital city of the country, and Sài Gòn a business capital. Statistics show that seven million people reside in Hà Nội and eight million in Sài Gòn. The real numbers are much higher than that. These cities are a little way south on the list of top fifty most populous cities in the world. Intimacy culture is something you could find in them in abundance alongside its twin sister, mega culture.

The symbolic image of Sài Gòn when I visited it in 2012 was the Bitexco Financial Tower. It was built by a French company and opened in October 2010. Its chief architect is the world-renown Venezuelan Carlos Zapata. Bitexco is a beautiful and iconic building in the world whose shape was drawn from inspiration of a lotus flower. 861 feet in height, it held the record as the tallest building in Vietnam, and the 124th in the world, for only a few months before it was topped in January 2011 by Keangnam Hanoi Landmark Tower of 1,132 feet and that was listed as the 37th highest in the world. In 2018, Bitexco dropped another notch as Landmark 81 rose. This 81-story building, at 1,513 feet high, constructed by a British architecture firm, is on the banks of the Sài Gòn river. It includes space for apartments, shopping centers, restaurants, hotels, bars and an observatory center. It broke the record as the highest observatory center and apartment building in Vietnam, the highest bar and restaurant in Southeast Asia, and the 14th tallest building in the world, as of July 2018, surpassing Kuala Lumpur's Petronas Towers and Chicago's Willis Tower. As architectural monuments are a sure sign of a thriving society, this vertical makeover of Vietnamese cities will continue, as many foreign journalists believe.

Other aspects of life are changing over there as well. Every time I visit Vietnam, I find its service industry breaking its own record and topping itself all over again. With the same amount of money spent in America, I receive five times more comfort and luxury in Vietnam. I was so spoiled by the friendliness of the people, by such delicious food and customer-oriented services everywhere, I kept coming back.

Everywhere I go, children are all around. They are annoying sometimes as they could be very loud. But they are only doing what kids are doing. This young population of Vietnamese is pumping their veins around to pull everybody else's instincts on their shoulders. This is the secret of the way people here live their lives— keeping the young blood flowing. Primitive could be the word that came to mind. And yet, it is this survival instinct kept active at appropriate level that is responsible for the youthful appearance of the people and the country. It keeps you on edge just enough to instill in you a daily dose of the happy thought that you do something right today to earn this existence. Just enough to keep the excitement on a leash.

It is amazing to think about all these things and imagine what optimal future Vietnam could have. I could get lost in this trend of thought. For a moment, I saw Vietnam as an old country yet so young; it makes America, a young country, look so old.

But human memory is short. After two months in Vietnam, I was saturated. I felt restless and unsettled. I missed my own bed in my Bloomington home. I missed the colorful garden and the citrus-like fragrance of the southern base magnolia flowers. And the gorgeous peonies whose magnificence no picture could capture. The orange azalea and the deep red Lucifer rhododendron. The pink roses and the purple lupines. The fish in the little pond. I missed the early morning in the yard void of human voices filled only with the sound of birds chirping and calling. And the deer taking refuge under the shade of the evergreen. I miss speaking English and the familiar orderly life.

20. TWO

"WHEN DO YOU COME BACK?" my friend in Vietnam messaged me on Facebook. She meant to ask when I was going to Vietnam for a visit.

"When do you come back?" a friend asked about my arrival time in California for Christmas.

Vietnamese people like to use the world 'back.' In their mind, Vietnam is still my home to come back to. Or home is where the Vietnamese community is—California.

Ever since I could remember, whenever I walked alone along the streets of Sài Gòn, the Vietnamese cyclo and xe ôm drivers called out to me in English thinking I was Korean or Japanese. Every single time. These days street vendors, merchants and strange men join the group. Many of them even think I am Chinese, the worst insult ever. I was already, and still am, not one of them in some way. The Vietnamese are clueless and undecided. I refuse to play this game as well.

At some point in my current life, 'back' became a vexing problem. It could even push me into a fit of pique when Vietnamese people refuse to recognize that Bloomington is my second home. In these moments, I seem to move away from 'we Vietnamese' and closer to 'they the Vietnamese.'

I looked forward to flying home.

Driving back from Indianapolis airport, as we got near Bloomington, I could not believe my eyes when the green cape spread along. It was even greener than in Vietnam where I formed my first memory of greenness. Bloomington was so green in a new way I never thought it could be. Distance does wonders to memory, I had to admit.

And yet, after a few months immobilized in Bloomington, I felt restless again. Suffocated even.

"Do you want to take me to school today?" my husband said as we were having breakfast.

He was not bored or anything. He was being a Bloomingtonian who is so spoiled he requests being driven to work instead of driving himself. His question and this situation could be oxymoron for an average American living in the car culture in the U.S.A and who worships his motorized independence to the T. That is not the case in Bloomington. Here, it is a luxury to be able to ask such a question on a daily basis. We live exactly three miles away from school and it takes ten minutes to get there. Along the small streets, hilly and windy, we yield to one another and a deer family trying to cross the street. It is a deer problem we have in this part of the country.

So it is not a strange question my husband asked. It does, however, reflect the quiet and off the beaten path location and culture of Bloomington. So quiet I feel as if I'm choking.

I miss the adrenaline pumping effects of life in my other homeland.

21. THREE

I VISITED VIETNAM AGAIN. BYPASSING SÀI GÒN, I escaped to
Đà Lạt.

Two hundred miles north of Sài Gòn, this used to be my childhood
haven for years, and a premium vacation spot fit for a king—Bảo
Đại built his summer palaces here. These days they are museums
open to public visits. As the school year came to an end, together
with my brothers and sister, I would pack and come to stay with
grandma for three summer months. Sneaking around four corners
of her garden hiding and seeking among the chayote vines, then
trekking the hills and the valleys, we built our memories of Đà Lạt.
We used to pick the perfectly shaped pine cones and stuff our pockets with them till the cones' edges poked through the fabric and
scratched us.

Thirty years from those days, the botanical gardens, the lakes,
the valleys and the waterfalls are pretty much unchanging, places
where the love games for the youngsters go on. Not feeling so much
pumped up, I went to look for my new memories of Đà Lạt on foot.
Along the winding hilly roads, red-roofed houses popping up at
every corner unexpectedly dot the hills, and spread on, creating a
canvas of abstract nature on which my imagination can stroll freely.
There, in the quiet of the scenery, I could hear my own feelings and
thoughts. From a distance, the inner child emerged, almost visible

on the abstract canvas in front of me. She was connecting the dots and having a great time. She was home.

I have been fortunate to have three hometowns. These physical and emotional journeys among them seem to have become the bulk of my life. A story here, an encounter there, a visit somewhere else, a déjà vu out of the blue moon. I have become a traveler who moves back and forth in space and time easing into places called home.

22. FOUR

ONE DAY IN VIETNAM I realized that, when chatting with my friends, I switched to English once in a while. Many other conversations I had with them were mostly in English because they preferred it that way. Still other times, we all mixed English and Vietnamese.

Language carries too many things for me.

In Vietnamese the talks about the past reeked of romanticism—nineteenth century French romanticism. This is one enduring impact of French colonialism on the locals that the Hollywood block busters could not erase. It evokes a sense of nostalgia and entitlement. Even when the topic is 'current affairs,' the Vietnamese use a romantic language that emits the kind of forgetfulness and privilege so desirable in a world where they believe that power belongs to the haves but time and memory belong to everyone. A solace in the storm for someone. Not me.

I'd rather create new time and new memory. I'd rather joke and curse in Vietnamese with my husband, using words we assign new meanings to. Or chat in English about theories we made up.

Or fight by writing in Vietnamese because English is not enough.

At times, admittedly, as if Vietnamese was too raw and naked, I found comfort in English.

To take cover, to get high, to create, or to fight, languages help me get rid of the sharpness of my desires to achieve more refined and focused attention. They've become a powerful means to spearhead my reality. I embed in them a story here and a memory there. Things of my time. They become pockets where I store secrets in life. They become another home.

* * *

At one point, I even believed I must somehow finalize something with both America and Vietnam to unify my four homes. My need for closure goes beyond the addressing issue of 'us' and 'them.'

Being different in America, visually at least in white Americans' view, I have already found writing as an outlet to affirm my identity. I have no qualms or scruples about being Vietnamese in America. And how could it be when, it is true that many Vietnamese traditions pushed me away, Vietnam is still my original homeland where I spent almost thirty years of my life. It is a huge part of my self and the attachment is undeniable and unbreakable. It is absolutely natural for me to fall back to it, or to fall for it all over again and again a hundred percent, and forget about everything else. It is natural for me to be a Vietnamese no matter where I live. But then that was unfair to my new homeland, I reasoned.

Is being a Vietnamese in America the same as being a Vietnamese American? I could not figure out how much of Vietnam I should allow myself to carry with me so as not to jeopardize my duty and obligation to my adopted homeland. I imagined a closure to Vietnam to be like achieving a half-half deal, meaning I divided myself half American-half Vietnamese; as if a closure was a door that once I close one side I open the other. A closure to Vietnam meant I was willing to be half-Vietnamese. It sounded silly; at the same time it was a sacrifice I believed I had to make for my life in America. I have been fretting about what it meant to be a Vietnamese American living in the U.S. and what was a right thing to do.

I looked around to find answers. Most Vietnamese Americans I knew, read, or read about are traumatized or influenced by the Vietnam War at different levels of intensity. Many of them, upon arriving in the U.S., expressed gratitude to the new land. They were happy to have survived in one piece and ready to start a new life. They felt indebted to America. They categorized themselves, or being done so by researchers, into the first, the one and a half, or the second generation, each group carrying with them certain identity traits they acknowledged, or they did not. It is a complicated analysis and discussion about the Vietnamese refugees and/or immigrants and how they lived and fit in American society.

I took a different turn to get here. I was armed with a different kind of baggage and don't fit in many of their versions of Vietnamese Americans. Those kinds of views and information were helpful to know but they still left me in abeyance waiting to be fully activated.

On my own, was I able to commit to being half-American as I imagined the citizenship deal to be like? What did it even mean, anyway, to be half-half like that? Not like Vietnam is America's buddy the way France, the UK, or Germany is. Over there, Vietnam is a completely different world. A comfortable balance between here and there was a long stretch. To find a middle point between the two places and hang myself on it so that I was equally distanced and fair to both was not a feasible solution.

But that was exactly what I was doing, living suspended between the two places determined to finalize the dividing line—just to find out in the end that there was none.

The half-half formula did not work. In spite of my effort to separate the shared identity of Vietnamese-American into different compartments—because I thought it might make my life easier, physical and emotional allegiance does not work that way. The Vietnamese and American parts in me mingle and interact. They borrow from and share with each other intricately. They evolve together. After a while, it is so hard to tell them apart.

In the multi-dimensional world we are these days, allegiance probably has its moments, or should I say universes. I just have to figure out for myself when and where.

I accept drifting between the two spaces waiting for the resolution to come.

Enlightenment is a state of mind. Maybe home could be so, too. Then, is this my fifth home? The Ultimate one?

ACKNOWLEDGMENTS

IN MANY WAYS, THIS BOOK started writing itself the moment I arrived in the U.S. with a scholarship to pursue higher education. I thank Donald Holsinger and Brigham Young University in Provo for this dream opportunity in life. I thank him again, together with Ignacio Garcia, Neil York, and Valerie Hudson for their wise counsels and unflinching support when I was exploring my paradise. I'm thankful to the History Department at Indiana University in Bloomington for the three years of scholarship.

My journey in America started with my big family in Aurora, Colorado. I thank every single one of them for their generosity and love. Their help and support the first two years were crucial for my overall well-being: cô Ba and bác Vinh—their memory will be with me always, chú Tô, cô Vân, mấy chị Như, Mai, Trâm, Trang, Nga, các anh Tốp, Phanh, Thôi, and their significant others, and my cousins Mi and Bo. I'm equally thankful to my second big family: chú Sim and cô Hồng, cô Nhuận and Leo. Final thanks to the Provo families: bác Bá and bác gái, Chi, and Đức.

Thank you to my editor, Michael Mirolla, for his very thoughtful edits and the whole Guernica team for help in bringing this book to the world.

This book would have taken much longer to arrive had it not been for Ignacio Garcia. I'm forever grateful for his mentorship and friendship. He read the first draft and provided much needed encouragements and insightful comments that eventually gave depth and shape to this book as it is. He read the last draft to give it the final push to send it on its own journey. Thanks to Viet Thanh Nguyen for reading five original chapters. His questions and comments helped shape this book more than he knew. Thank you Henry Cooper for reading and commenting on two original chapters. Sandra Freund read the first draft and sent along encouragement and enthusiasm. She is my cheerleader. Thanks Sandra.

I thank my friends in Sài Gòn, Hà Hương and Kim Chi, for hosting me during my research trip in 2012. They were an inspiration.

I am indebted to my father, Thiết Thạch Hoàng, and my mother, Thu-Cúc Cao. Their sacrifice and love after the war years made it possible for me to feel that, in spite of the hardships, I was wrapped in love and safety my entire childhood. I am who I am today because of them. Thanks to my sister, Temy Hoàng and her husband, Steve Giamporcaro, and my brothers, Luân Thạch Hoàng and Hoàng Thạch Quân, for their unconditional love and support.

Thank you to my soul mate, P.Q. Phan. Everything starts with you.

ABOUT THE AUTHOR

ANVI HOÀNG GREW UP IN Vietnam. She taught ESL for six years before coming to the U.S. for graduate studies. After a stint in the academy that culminated in an MA degree in American Studies, another one in American History, and still another in Public Health, she found peace in creative writing. Anvi has travelled extensively in the U.S., Europe and Asia. The cultural observations have made her life all the more fluid. In 2015 she co-founded and has since managed a non-profit organization, the Vietnamese American Society for Creative Arts and Music (VASCAM). She has collaborated with her husband, P.Q. Phan, and become co-lyricist of an art song, *Phở*, and co-librettist of a chamber opera, *What the Horse Eats*. *Why Do You Look at Me and See a Girl?* is her debut book.